WARWICKSHIRE COLLEGE
* 0 0 5 1 6 7 7 8 *

LIBRARY
WARWICKSHIRE
COLLEGE

A Tiger's Tale

A Tiger's Tale

The Indian Tiger's Struggle for Survival in the Wild

ANUP & MANOJ SHAH

Designed by Grant Bradford

FOUNTAIN PRESS

Published by
Fountain Press Limited
2 Gladstone Road, Fountain House
Kingston-upon-Thames, Surrey KT1 3HD, England

Design and Illustrations by Grant Bradford
Origination by Erayscan, Singapore
Printing & Binding by Vallardi, milan
ISBN 9 780863 433917

For Neha, Mansi and Devang

DECLARATION

All the photographs of tigers and other animals presented in this book were taken in Ranthambhore Forest, India, under totally free, natural and uncontrolled conditions. In addition, in no way whatsoever has any of the images been either digitally or mechanically manipulated. These are pure photographs.

FRONTISPIECE

Having fed, Laxmi's two adolescent daughters Bela and Choti enjoy a lie-in. Note that their entire bodies, save for the heads, are immersed in water. It has been repeatedly observed that tigers do not like getting their faces wet.

Noorjahan walking on leaf-strewn forest track.

Preface

In the romantic Indian state of Rajasthan there is a fabulous forest, Ranthambhore. It has a special place in the hearts and minds of many people. The fond memories of Ranthambhore and its inhabitants transcends everyday life. This book is an attempt to relate, in words and photographs, that exhilarating encounter with another world.

Ranthambhore is a small gem of a national park. As early as the 1960s, visitors "in the know" used to go there. In the late 70s and early 80s, word got around and this trickle of visitors became a flood; for the Ranthambhore experience, all one had to do was hire a jeep and drive through the park. In winter you wrapped up warm before boarding the open jeep and wondered if it was worth it. Invariably you came back from the game drive highly charged, all thoughts of the cold banished from body and soul. In summer it was like an oven. You returned parched yet hardly aware of it. The animals made you forget such things.

The forest has more than its share of sambar and chital deer. There are antelopes too - nilgai and chinkara - and the primate associated with India, the common langur. It is home to the national bird - the peacock - and another native, the painted stork. But however rich this variety, non-predators don't move many people. For excitement, for emotional thrill there is one sovereign, the world's finest mammal. And once upon a time they roamed here, the tigers of Ranthambhore.

Contents

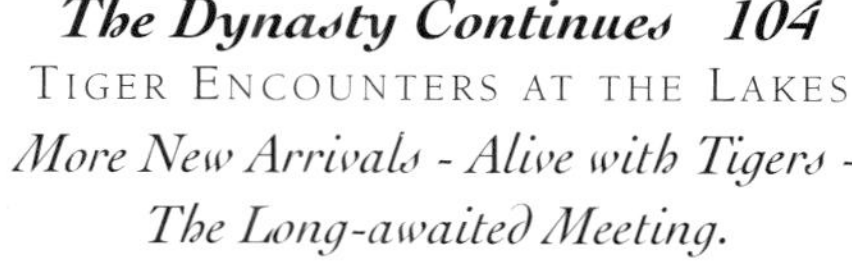

Ranthambhore

CONSERVATION AND NATURAL HISTORY OF A WORLD FAMOUS TIGER RESERVE

Indian Conservation History

The origins of India's protected areas can, ironically, be traced to the passion of the Mogul Emperors for hunting. In order to safeguard their hunting interests, the Moguls enforced protection laws and, following an old Persian tradition, introduced game preserves. The Moguls hunted with primitive weapons but the arrival of the British in India coincided with technical advancement in firearms. Hunting was a popular sport amongst British army officers and civil servants as well as Indian Maharajahs and princes. But it was also during the British colonial rule that further moves towards conservation in India took place. One measure built upon the Mogul game preserves by establishing 'reserved forest' blocks and hunting by permit only. The second was the setting up of national parks and sanctuaries. India's first national park was established in 1936.

Tiger Alarm

Independence, won in 1947, did not bring any relief for the tiger; in fact pressure increased. While under the British there had been some control over hunting, now the British game laws were flouted and India was gripped by a hunting orgy that took years to bring under control. At the same time, human population grew and the accompanying habitat destruction turned out to be a major destroyer of wildlife. During the 1950s the cheetah became extinct in India and in the 1960s it was realized that the tiger was probably destined for the same fate.

Action to Save the Tiger

The spur to action was a census carried out in 1972 which revealed that India's tiger population had dropped from an estimated 40,000 early this century to around 1,800. The Indian Government passed the Wildlife (Protection) Act and, together with Nepal and the World Wide Fund for Nature, launched an international appeal to save the big cat.

Project Tiger

Project Tiger was formally launched on 1st April 1973 and proved to be a turning point in Indian wildlife conservation. Its first step was to abolish the tiger shikar (hunt). The second was to save the tiger's habitat. Accordingly, a variety of wild habitats throughout the Indian sub-continent were turned into protected areas. The tiger population recovered swiftly - by 1988 the number of tigers was estimated to have doubled - and in the process many other animals received protection as well.

Ranthambhore's History

Ranthambhore, in the state of Rajasthan, was one of the initial nine reserves to be brought under the Project Tiger programme. This wasn't surprising since Ranthambhore's fame as a tiger ilaka (area) dates back many centuries. Ancient kings, armed with primitive weapons, sought out the tigers. When not pursuing this dangerous pastime, they defended their kingdom from the fort which overlooks the forest. (Ranthambhore derives its name from this fort). From the records we know that the fort was already in existence in the 11th century, then the centre of a Hindu kingdom. Wars were fought as the fort changed hands between the Moguls and the Rajputs several times.

A view from the nearby escarpment of Ranthambhore's famous lakes and the equally famous rest-house of Jogi Mahal. The park is clearly seen to be surrounded by low hills.

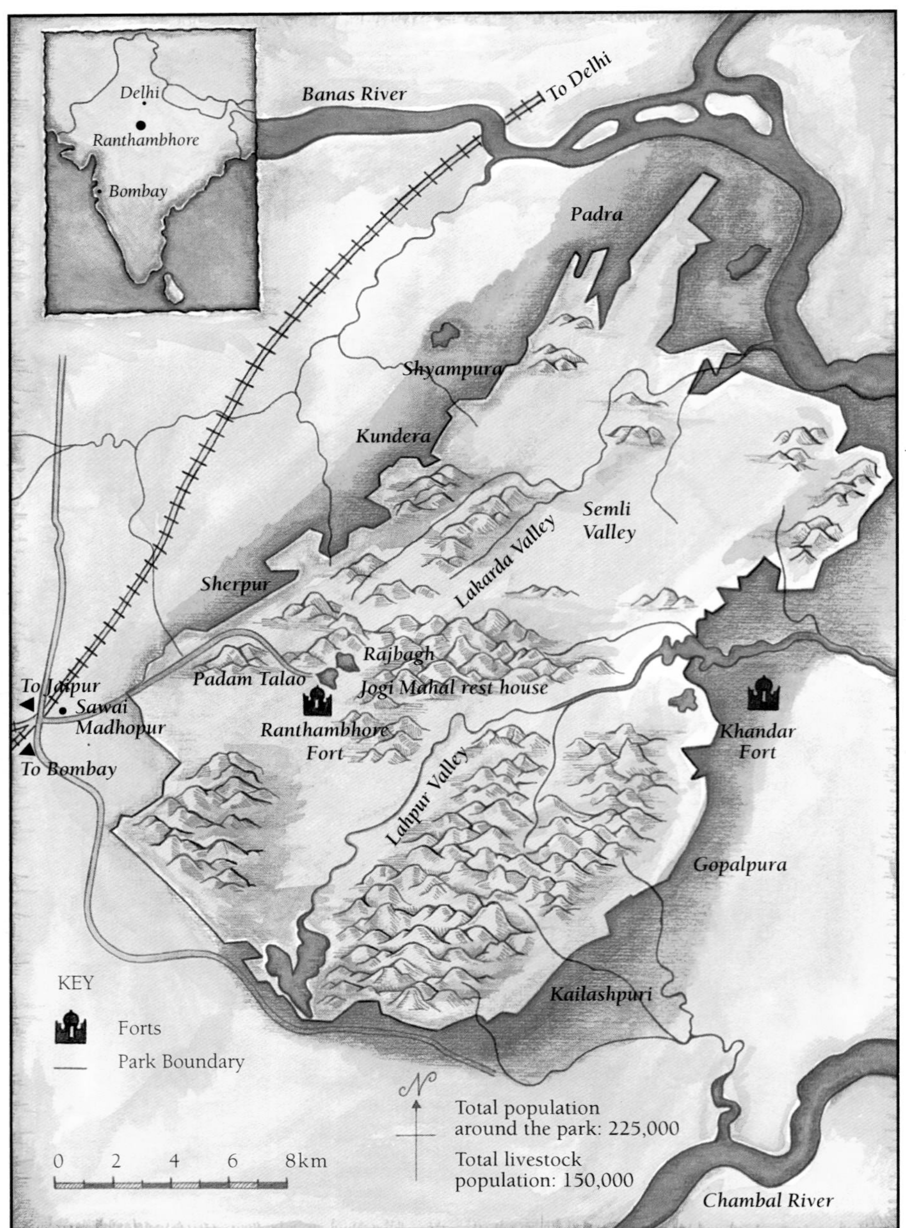

Ranthambhore National Park

Ranthambhore as a Protected Area

Before the post-independence government of India stepped in, the fort was in the hands of the Maharajahs of Jaipur who utilized the forest as a hunting ground. Although they tried to keep tiger shoots to a minimum, and despite in 1957 Ranthambhore being given protection as a wildlife sanctuary, tiger numbers steadily decreased. In 1972, as part of the nation-wide census, it was estimated that Ranthambhore had only 14 tigers. However, it is likely that without the protection afforded by the Maharajahs, the tiger situation in Ranthambhore would have been even worse.

Ranthambhore - Project Tiger

After Ranthambhore was incorporated in the Project Tiger Programme, the first task was to relocate ten villages outside the reserve boundary and between 1976-79, twelve villages that had existed within the reserve were resettled outside. In 1981 Ranthambhore was declared a national park, free of human disturbance. The tiger numbers recovered and the 1987 census found them to have tripled to 42.

Ranthambhore - Natural History

Today, Ranthambhore is one of the smallest of 18 Project Tiger reserves. It is a dry deciduous forest that extends to 392 sq. km. The geology of Ranthambhore is dominated by the Aravalli and the Vindhyan hills and the rock is mostly limestone, sandstone and shale. The vegetation is dominated by dhok trees and there is a sprinkling of ancient banyan and peepal trees. The spreading roots of the banyan are particularly eye-catching. Mango trees are scattered all over the park and there are evergreen strips with abundant jamun trees that streak across the forest. There is refreshing permanent water and the temperatures are markedly cooler, providing a welcome respite to tigers during the uncomfortable hot months. Traversing across the park, the scenery is frequently interrupted by huge rock formations, steep escarpments, large lakes and small streams.

Adolescent langur monkeys playing around an ancient banyan tree. Langur monkeys, also known as Hanuman monkeys, are a characteristic primate species of India and are plentiful in Ranthambhore. Acrobatic, agile and social, a troop is often amusing to watch.

Riding in a cart pulled by a camel, the villagers return at dusk from the nearby town of Sawai Madhopur. Their village is one of many sited just outside Ranthambhore.

The forest also occasionally opens out into large areas of grassland. A unique touch to Ranthambhore is given by the littering of the forest with the remnants of its historic past: old defensive walls, ancient step wells, cupolas, guard posts, mosques, memorial stones and other structures all bear mute testimony to kingdoms and battles. Overgrown now, they blend with their natural surroundings. Tigers are sometimes seen roaming about in these ancient ruins.

Ranthambhore Seasons

During the monsoon season, July to September, the forest has a lush green veil and the lakes and streams overflow with water. Animals are found scattered all over the park. In sharp contrast, at the onset of summer in April, the forest is shrunk and shrivelled and most of the streams and water holes have run dry. The height of summer is in May when the temperature reaches 45°centigrade (in the winter months of January the temperature often falls to freezing). The dun landscape hurts the eye. This is the 'pinch period' and animals are generally found concentrated around the remaining water supplies. This is also the time when the annual census is carried out.

Looking towards the escarpment and the ruins of the once magnificent Ranthambhore fort.

Wildlife

The plant species list for the park includes about 300 trees, 50 aquatic plants and over 100 herbs, grasses, climbers and seasonal plants. Many bird-watching groups visiting India include Ranthambhore in their itinerary since the bird list exceeds 275 species. The number of reptiles and amphibian species is comfortably in double figures as is the number of fish species. No one has yet catalogued the wide variety of insects found here. And there are also the mammals, at least 22 different species which, by Indian standards, is a highly respectable number. The list, of course, includes tigers and over the course of six years we must have identified at least 40 different individuals.

Noorjahan within the lakes landscape. Notice that the terrain is relatively open, making tigers more visible in Ranthambhore than elsewhere in India.

The Tiger

PORTRAIT OF AN ENDANGERED PREDATOR

The tiger is the largest living cat. Its power and strength are legendary - numerous stories abound of a tiger jumping over village walls with a bullock carried in its jaws. Armed with long canine teeth it is a fearsome adversary in the wild and there is a true account of a tiger battling an elephant in the night and emerging as the victor in the morning. This massively built animal is also amazingly graceful, best exemplified when it sinuously moves in the jungle, giving the impression of gliding. There is also no doubt that it is exceedingly beautiful and its big moist eyes and exquisitive markings tempt many people to want to cuddle this big cat. The eyes also hint at keen intelligence and the cat is cunning, repeatedly outwitting prey and humans alike. Not surprisingly, the tiger is the ruler of the jungle and it shows - when it is on a prowl the atmosphere is charged, the air crackles and the denizens of the jungle are on full alert. Proud and aloof, as befitting royalty, the tiger has no friends in the wild.

Physique

The tiger is a huge animal with powerful muscles. The record is of a male weighing 384 kg. The tiger's physique reflects adaptations for the capture and killing of large prey. The hindlimbs are longer than the forelimbs as an adaptation for jumping: the forelimbs and shoulders are very muscular - much more so than the hindlimbs - and the forepaws are equipped with long, sharp retractile claws, enabling them to snatch and subdue prey. The head is rounded and catlike and the skull is foreshortened, thereby increasing the shearing leverage of the powerful jaws. A killing bite is swiftly delivered by the long, somewhat flattened canines.

Senses

The tiger can see at great distances and the design of the eyes also gives it a wide-angle view. But the resolving power is not great so that the tiger has difficulty in seeing motionless objects. On the other hand, its night vision is excellent, easily surpassing that of the prey animals that it hunts. The tiger's sense of smell, however, is weak. Although a tiger can extract a great deal of information by sniffing an object sprayed upon by another tiger, it is unlikely that a tiger can detect the scent of human beings. Moreover, tigers do not appear to use the sense of smell to find prey. The tiger's hearing is highly developed - it can distinguish between a leaf rustling in the breeze and one brushed by another animal. The tiger's whiskers also serve as a sensory organ - at night when the whiskers brush against vegetation, the tiger can judge its position in relation to other objects.

Locomotion

The tiger walks smoothly, due to the almost simultaneous movement of both the legs on one side of the body and then the other. It also moves silently, the pads of the tiger's feet being surprisingly soft. However, they are also sensitive and can be easily burnt or grazed. Trained observers can glean much information - such as sex, age, weight - by studying a tiger's pug-mark (paw-print). For such a heavy animal, the tiger can run fast, covering up to 4 metres at a bound, though it cannot keep up its sprint for more than 100 metres. It can also jump well - there are instances of leaps of 6 metres across and 2 metres high. Tigers can climb trees and cubs often play in trees. They are also strong swimmers and can swim for over 5,000 metres at a stretch.

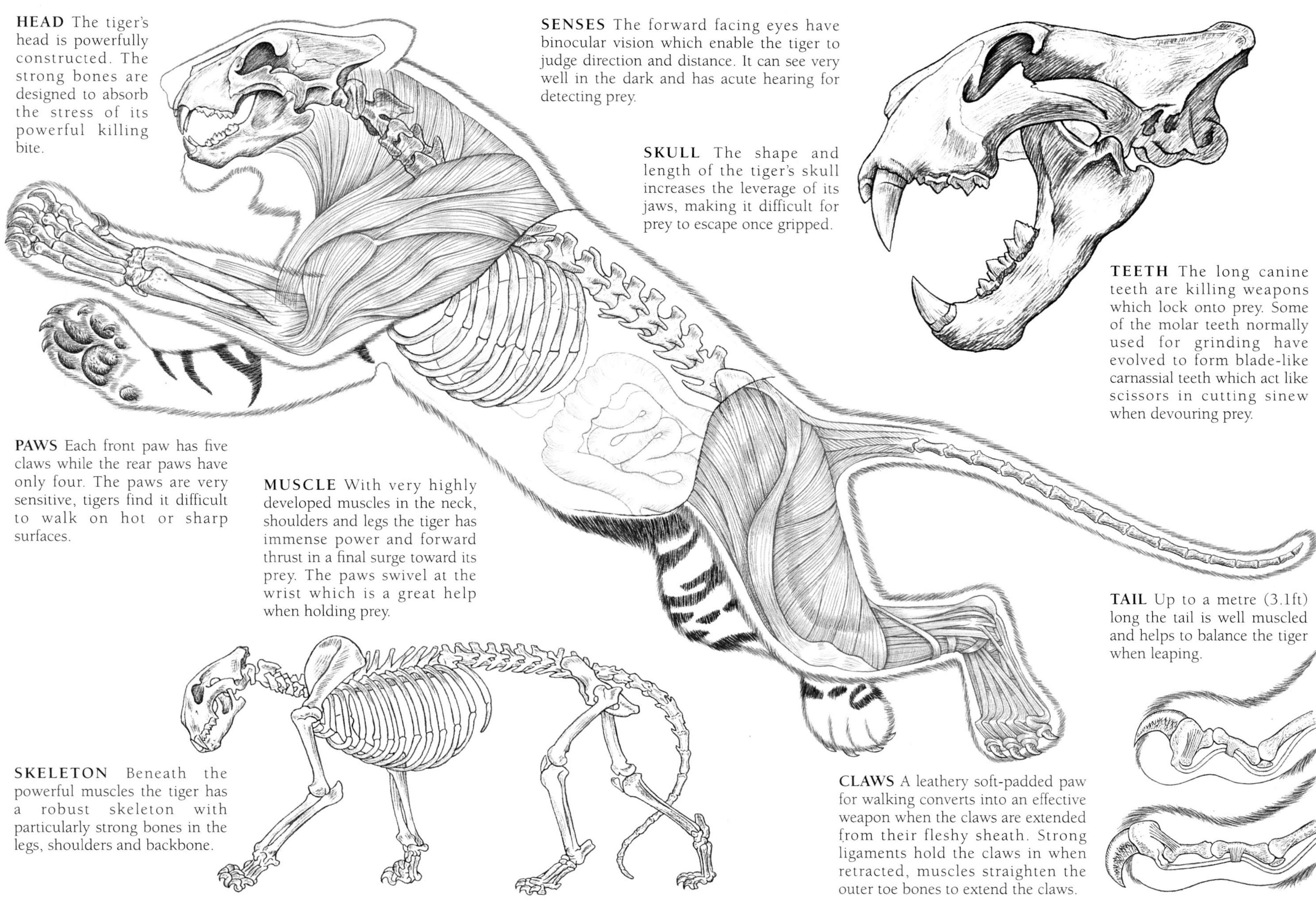

HEAD The tiger's head is powerfully constructed. The strong bones are designed to absorb the stress of its powerful killing bite.

SENSES The forward facing eyes have binocular vision which enable the tiger to judge direction and distance. It can see very well in the dark and has acute hearing for detecting prey.

SKULL The shape and length of the tiger's skull increases the leverage of its jaws, making it difficult for prey to escape once gripped.

TEETH The long canine teeth are killing weapons which lock onto prey. Some of the molar teeth normally used for grinding have evolved to form blade-like carnassial teeth which act like scissors in cutting sinew when devouring prey.

PAWS Each front paw has five claws while the rear paws have only four. The paws are very sensitive, tigers find it difficult to walk on hot or sharp surfaces.

MUSCLE With very highly developed muscles in the neck, shoulders and legs the tiger has immense power and forward thrust in a final surge toward its prey. The paws swivel at the wrist which is a great help when holding prey.

TAIL Up to a metre (3.1ft) long the tail is well muscled and helps to balance the tiger when leaping.

SKELETON Beneath the powerful muscles the tiger has a robust skeleton with particularly strong bones in the legs, shoulders and backbone.

CLAWS A leathery soft-padded paw for walking converts into an effective weapon when the claws are extended from their fleshy sheath. Strong ligaments hold the claws in when retracted, muscles straighten the outer toe bones to extend the claws.

Origins

The popular image of the tiger is that of a striped cat prowling in a tropical jungle, but in fact it originates from Siberia. About 10,000 years ago, the tiger began to spread out as fluctuations in ice cover made many of its original habitats unsuitable for living. At the same time, the numbers and varieties of herbivores elsewhere increased. Eventually, tigers occupied nearly all the sub-tropical and tropical parts of Asia where there was prey.

Tiger Races

Tigers from the original northern habitat are the largest - the Siberian tiger measuring up to 4 metres in length-and they have long shaggy fur in keeping with a cold climate. Their coat colour is paler than that of the Southern races. Further South, the Bengal tiger is smaller with a length of 3 metres and the average male weighs 200 kg., the average female 140 kg. In the extreme South of the tiger's range, the island races are the smallest of all and their general colouration is dark, with narrowing striping and short fur.

In general, then, the tiger developed a gradual southwards change, from maximum to minimum average size and weight, from palest to darkest colouration and from longest to shortest fur.

Past and Present Distribution

Towards the beginning of the 20th century, the tiger's kingdom extended far and wide in Asia and it is estimated that there were hundreds of thousands of tigers. Eight different races (or subspecies) existed. The past and current status of these is as follows.

SIBERIAN TIGER *(Panthera tigris altaica)* / Russian Far East, China and North Korea.

Also known as the Amur tiger and sometimes referred to as the Manchurian tiger, the largest, heaviest and most powerful of the Tiger family. It has been on the endangered list for some time. In the 1930s, only 30 to 50 animals were known to exist in the wild. The estimated number in 1992 was 350-550. Since then the numbers have dramatically fallen.

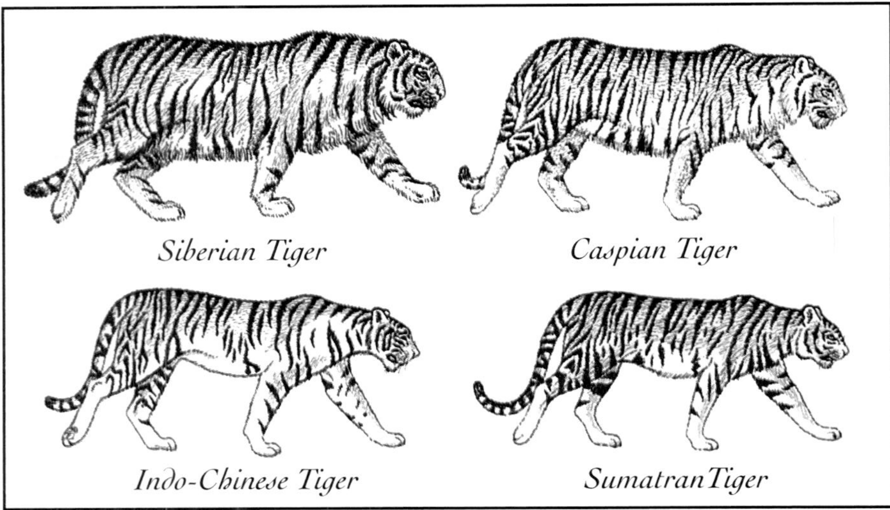

Comparative profiles of tiger species.

CHINESE TIGER *(Panthera tigris amoyensis)* / Central and South China.

A smaller tiger with a shorter coat than the Siberian. It was brought to the verge of extinction by an official campaign in the 1950s and 1960s to wipe it out because it was considered a pest. At least 3,000 tigers were killed. It has not been sighted recently but Chinese experts put the numbers at 30-50, widely scattered and critically endangered.

INDO-CHINESE TIGER *(Panthera tigris corbetti)* / Eastern Myanmar to Vietnam and Malaysia.

Also known as Corbett's tiger. Smaller than the Bengal tiger and darker in colour with short stripes. Although estimates of up to 2,000 have been published, there is no evidence to support this figure. The only reasonable estimate has been that of about 250 in Thailand in 1991.

SUMATRAN TIGER *(Panthera tigris sumatra)* / Sumatra Island.

Smaller than the Indo-Chinese tiger. Dark red in colour with cream-coloured areas. Long black stripes often in double layers. During the last 20 years, estimates have not been higher than 1,000 and Indonesian specialists currently think that there are 400-650 in five disjointed protected areas. Their future is highly uncertain.

A Plaster of Paris mould is easily made, it only takes half an hour and provides a permanent record. The individual tiger can be identified by its pug-mark features – shape, size, any abnormalities, etc. However, reliable pug-marks can be obtained only if the marks are very clear on the dirt track.

JAVAN TIGER *(Panthera tigris sondaica)* / Virtually extinct.

Named after its homeland, the Indonesian island of Java. Similar to the Sumatran but darker with more and closer-set black stripes. A dozen or so were known to exist in the 1950s. Last sightings were in 1981. Tiger scratch marks on a tree were spotted in 1990. Since then, there has been no signs of this species.

CASPIAN TIGER *(Panthera tigris virgata)* / Virtually extinct.

Roamed the Westernmost range to Afghanistan, Iran, the Caspian and Turkey. Similar in size and colour to the Bengal tiger. Could a few still be surviving in a remote part of Afghanistan?

BALI TIGER *(Panthera tigris balica)* / Extinct.

Another Indonesian island tiger. It was darker and had fewer stripes than the other Indonesian tigers. The last survivor was reported to have been shot in 1937.

Each tiger face or 'mask' is as individual as a human face. The stripes, markings, shape of ears and mane are a distinctive means of identification. A family tree of the tigers described in this book is on page 133.

INDIAN TIGER *(Panthera tigris tigris)* / Indian Sub-continent, Western Myanmar, possibly Tibet.

Also known as the Bengal tiger. Medium-sized tiger with short, glossy coat. Estimates of 250 in three populations in Nepal and 150 in Bhutan appear exaggerated. Bangladesh may have about 200. No estimates are available for Myanmar. Together with a highly generous estimate of 2,500 in India, that makes for an optimistic total of 3,000.

Like other countries, India had many more tigers in the past. There were then vast areas of suitable habitat and human population densities were lower.

Enter Ashoka

THE FIRST SIGHTINGS OF NALGHATI FEMALE AND HER CUBS

One minute there was nothing on the track, the next there was a tiger. Searching for wildlife is full of surprises, when you have tried everything and just as you resign yourself to yet another hopeless attempt, something happens, a tiger appears and, as an added bonus, stays.

She emerged from the forest which lies on either side of the vehicle track. Fully grown and in peak condition, relaxed yet watchful. As we admired her we were rewarded with another surprise. A tiger cub, about 4 months old, appeared. He went up to nuzzle his mother who was watching us candidly. The tigress could not have been in any particular hurry for she settled down in front of our jeep, relaxed but still facing us. Over the months we came to realize that tigers often do this: if, while walking, they come across a jeep, they take the opportunity of a rest. For a few minutes they sit down, look around, yawn, groom themselves and then resume their walk. It must be wonderful to savour life like that, untroubled by time.

When it rains it really pours. Lurking in the forest, torn between fear and family companionship, was the tigress's female cub. She brought herself hesitantly to the track's edge. Her movements caught the ear of her brother, who bounded up and began a playful scrap. He soon tired of this, however, and rejoined his mother on the track. Perhaps vigorous playing had made his sister bolder for she, too, walked towards her mother, watching us closely. She hissed a little, growled and finally, after a warning snarl, rubbed heads with her mother and sat down, fixing us with an unblinking stare.

So that's the way it was : the forest, the three tigers and our jeep. The tranquil scene held for several minutes before the tigress rose and strolled along the track. The cubs kept her in sight as they picked out their own routes behind her. They gambolled a little, sniffed interesting objects, and poked their heads into crevices. We followed at a discreet distance but eventually lost them, something we were fated to do repeatedly in the future. This is the maddening aspect of tiger watching - just as things are getting interesting the tigers tend to disappear.

The Problem of Names

We called the tigress Nalghati Female, Nalghati being the area she occupied. Naming tigers after the areas they occupy is not definitive since, in the course of their lives, most tigers change areas. You might name a tiger after a distinct behavioural characteristic, but it takes much more time to get to know a tiger and isolate what makes it unique. In fact, Nalghati Female had a nick in her right ear and some people did refer to her as "Nick-ear" but this led to some confusion because there was another tigress living in Bakola area who also had a nicked ear. (How could they have got these marks? Perhaps it is an injury sustained during vigorous mating with an over enthusiastic male. Interestingly, we have yet to come across any sub-adult tigers with cuts in their ears.)

Returning to the problem of names, it is often solved by time. A tiger in Ranthambhore initially gets a temporary name which is then adopted by so many people that it becomes permanent.

Nalghati Female's mother was called Padmini, after a Hindu goddess, and her home range took in Nalghati Valley and the adjoining lakes. In 1981 Padmini was seen with three cubs. The two females were Nalghati Female and Noon, so called because she often hunted at midday. Nobody knows what happened to the male cub and Padmini herself disappeared in 1983 and the two adjacent areas of her home range, Nalghati Valley and the lakes, came to be occupied by Nalghati Female and Noon respectively.

Kublai, the resident male of the Lakes-Nalghati Valley area, emerging from the cover of tall grass into dawn's golden light. He had spent the better part of the night feeding with the tigress called Noon and their two cubs. Of medium size and sleek in appearance Kublai was reticent in manner.

Nalghati Female sits relaxed on the dirt track but her female cub, Nalghati Beti, is betraying signs of nervousness. The little one soon settled down, however, no doubt taking cues from her mother's body language.

The first time visitor to Ranthambhore finds it easy to identify Nalghati Valley. Narrow and steepsided, its towering walls impart a real sense of wilderness. Dense vegetation makes animals difficult to see although their density is moderately high. In a few places water collects and persists. This is important for tigers, since they rarely stray away from a water source. With good cover to assist hunting, and numerous den sites, Nalghati Valley must be very attractive to a tigress.

A Tigress of the Imagination

We first encountered Nalghati Female in April 1986. She was strikingly mature - big, cool, observant and exuding latent power, like the tigress of one's imagination. Her two cubs born sometime in December 1985, seemed in capable hands. So we were surprised to learn that this was probably her first litter. Nalghati Female had used a luxuriant bush as her den site, well-hidden, virtually inaccessible, and near a small pool. The resident male tiger of Nalghati Valley and the adjoining lakes was Kublai. He was a medium-sized, sleek-looking tiger quite reticent in manner. Often observed interacting in a friendly manner with Nalghati Female and her cubs, he was almost certainly the father.

Observations such as that of the male tiger resting and feeding with his tigress and cubs were rare even in 1986. The history of tiger observation prior to 1986, apart from two notable research projects, was a collection of scattered glimpses and nocturnal viewing at bait sites. Lengthy natural observations were scarce and as a result, several misconceptions prevailed. One was the tiger's supposed inflexibility - a creature of very strict behavioural rules from which it seldom deviated. For instance, people thought it rarely hunted before dusk or after dawn. However, as we shall see, the tiger is highly flexible. It changes its habits and behaviour since the focus of all its instincts is survival, which necessitates adaptability. One of our aims in this book is to up-date the image of this professional predator.

Nalghati Female, accompanied by her vibrant male cub, Ashoka, pauses while walking on a forest track. It was just after seven in the morning when we chanced upon this magnificent tigress with her two four month old cubs. Capable, confident, graceful and lethal, she epitomized the tigress of one's imagination.

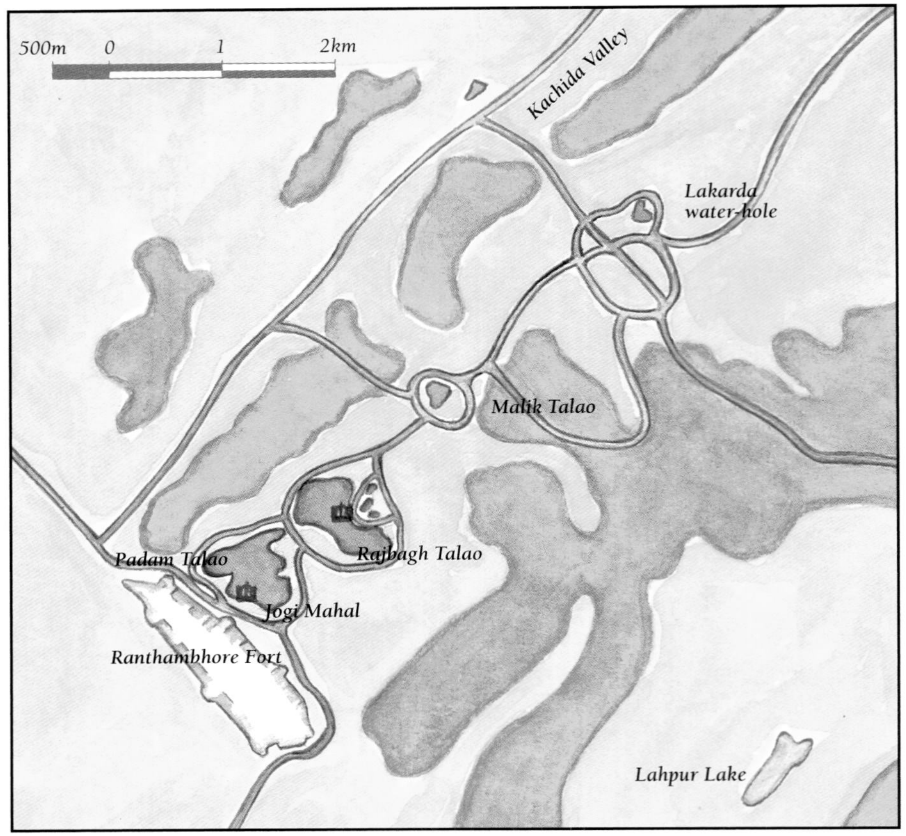

Ranthambhore, 1986

Consider Ranthambhore in 1986. In that exceptional year eight tigresses with 17 cubs were sighted (far more than in previous years). These tiger families were spread through the forest. Around picturesque Lahapur there was a tigress with 3 cubs. She was a shadowy figure and since very few people visited the area, her cubs were shy. At first sight of a vehicle, all four would disappear. Moving inwards into the park, there was Nalghati Female with her inquisitive son and shy daughter. Nalghati Female's living area shared a common border with the living area of two other tigresses. There was Adabalaji Female, living in Adabalaji area beyond the park gate. Her densely vegetated range straddled the main road leading to the Park. She was able to skulk at will but one occasionally spotted her with her two cubs, a male and a female.

Ranthambhore's legendary track number 2 starts at the park gate and cuts through diverse habitats. The track became famous for its tigers and in 1986 one could easily spot three tigresses each with cubs along its length. The resident tigress of the lakes, which lie on the edge of the park's core area, was Noon, Nalghati Female's sister. Her two cubs were born in May 1986 and evidence pointed again to Kublai as the father. Driving past the Lakes one soon came to the Lakarda area where resident tigress, Laxmi, was occupying a remote corner, Semli Valley. Small and pretty, it was home to Laxmi's three irrepressible cubs. Adjacent to Semli was Bakola, a miniature gorge, dramatic and colourful. Bakola Ben, the resident tigress, had no cubs in 1986 but she gave birth to two cubs in early 1987. The explosion in cub numbers extended beyond Bakola, for at Dundermal Ka Dhera there was yet another tigress with two cubs. Returning to the park entrance taking track number 1 there was a fair chance of encountering Kachida Female with her three cubs. However, sightings of this particular tigress were infrequent - partly because track number 1 is monotonous, and most people chose track 2.

The Essentials of Tiger Life

Why this explosion in tiger numbers? A plausible answer is that the tigresses of Ranthambhore were well-settled in stable home ranges, which is conducive to breeding. The essentials of life for a female tiger are food, water, and den sites and the division of these basics between individual tigresses depends on the distribution of available prey animals. In Ranthambhore, prey density is high so that the home ranges of the tigresses are small. However, prey animals do scatter during the three months of monsoon rains. The tigers disperse too, reverting to their well-defined living areas after the monsoons.

In 1986, the basic social pattern was this: each of the eight tigresses had her own home range - which is not the same as territory. What is the difference between these two terms? Imagine you are following Nalghati Female. You sense a definite purpose in her habitual movements. She takes in well-defined hunting places, drinking spots, resting sites and vantage points. And as she moves over and over again through the same places it is as if her movements are linking them up. Thus her living area becomes discernible and zoologists refer to this as a "home range". The other term, stricter in usage, is "territory". Nalghati Female did not bother to defend the whole of her home range from intruding tigresses but she had a core area, which took in a permanent water hole, that she defended actively. This core area was her territory. Why did Nalghati Female not defend her entire home range? Perhaps, as her home range was much larger than her territory, it was just not worth it in terms of energy and time.

Kublai on a territorial patrol.

Laxmi, the resident female of the Lakarda area. Like her younger sister Noon, Laxmi was frequently sighted. Cool, calm and collected she was approachable in a vehicle. A tigress to admire.

The Male Situation

Nalghati Female tolerated Kublai, the male tiger, within her territory. The male tiger, unlike the adult tigress who is preoccupied with the rearing of her young, is motivated by the powerful urge to mate. To maximise his mating chances, the home range of a male tiger may often overlap with the home ranges of two, three and occasionally even more tigresses. This, of course, is feasible if the home ranges of the tigresses are small to begin with. The high prey density in Ranthambhore ensured this. Thus Kublai's turf took in the home ranges of Nalghati Female, Noon, and Adabalaji Female. There was a male with a cut tail in attendance at Lahapur and another male frequented Kachida Valley. Beyond Kachida Valley a huge male took in the areas of Bakola, Dundermal Ka Dhera and Lakarda. Thus there were four males taking in at least eight tigresses and it is interesting to note that their home ranges overlapped only fractionally - clearly the males did not tolerate each other being too close - although we cannot recall any instance in which any of them was called upon to defend his pitch aggressively. Normally a Ranthambhore male signals to the others that his area is under active occupation by regularly leaving 'occupied' signs - scent

Bakola Ben, the resident female of Bakola area. Bakola Ben exhuded placidity. However, when on a hunt, she personified tenacity, ferocity and raw, brutal power. A tigress to stand in awe of.

marks - throughout the area. Since these fade with time, a tiger moving into a strange area is able to tell whether it is occupied, by the freshness of the scent.

Breeding and Sightings

Why were so many tigresses breeding? The answer probably lay in the stability of the tigers' land tenure system, for stability confers two considerable advantages on resident tigresses. First, by marking an area off for herself and discouraging other tigresses from using it, she reduces competition, and therefore conflict. Second, she comes to know the best places to hunt at different times of the year, where the best rest sites are, and where to find water in the dry seasons. These two advantages are sizeable for a breeding tigress because tiger cubs depend solely on their mother for food. They do not have permanent canine teeth with which to apply the fatal bite and so cannot hunt successfully. Even after 1 year, when the permanent canines are in place, it takes another six months for the young tiger to dispatch small prey. So for a year and a half, the mother kills for her cubs. Consequently, the survival of the whole family depends on a tigress's hunting efficiency, plus prey availability, which in turn depends on a stable home range.

There is an additional question to that of explosion in cub numbers. Why did the tigers show themselves more to human observers? Generally speaking, wild animals have a natural inclination to avoid confrontation with humans whenever circumstances allow. Animals are concerned with their daily business of living and they may regard us as a hindrance. Also many animals have an in-built fear of humans, acquired through centuries of experience. But animals can overcome such inhibitions by a learning process called habituation. In Ranthambhore, the number of jeeps increased steadily from 1980 onwards. The jeeps did not threaten the tigers who became increasingly accustomed to their presence and gradually lost their fear. That wasn't sufficient reason for the tigers to give up the sanctuary of cover, though. Circumstances sometimes conspire to promote habituation. Now during hot weather, tigers are tempted to lie in cool water, even if the pool is out in the open, and it was thus that the tigers got 'caught'. One is, of course, trying to read a tiger's mind here and so we will probably never know the precise mechanism of habituation, only that tigers do get accustomed to humans in jeeps.

The Nalghati Family

Thus the Nalghati family grew up under the friendly eye of human observers protected from outside disturbances. Sustained observation was however difficult. A week could pass without a glimpse of any of the three. The problem was the terrain; a jeep is restricted to the single track cutting through Nalghati, and cover is plentiful everywhere in the valley. Therefore the tigers had most of the valley to themselves and could appear and disappear at will. Whenever they were spotted, they usually stayed awhile but sooner or later the family either climbed up a steep incline or disappeared into the dark nala of the valley.

From March through June, however, the movements of the family were confined to a narrow band of 2.5 sq. km. Water had evaporated in most places so Nalghati Female was concentrating on a couple of waterholes in the stretch. Deer and the occasional antelope were being drawn in towards the precious water here and so, for Nalghati Female, it was merely a matter of waiting in ambush. Although the prey animals were aware of her presence, they were severely restricted in their choice of water supply and consequently approached either of the two waterholes slowly and cautiously. During such advances they paused repeatedly to cock an ear, sniff the air, and try to peer through the cover. They showed signs of jumpiness and often fled at the

Noon, Nalghati Female's twin sister and the resident female of the Lakes area. Noon was so-called because she was often observed looking for prey at mid-day. Extremely tolerant of vehicles, except when on a kill, she was often visible. A tigress to respect.

slightest hint, real or imaginary, of danger. But their need for water eventually lured them to the water's edge. As soon as their mouths made contact with the water, they were hypnotized by the intoxicating relief that comes when a great thirst is being quenched. One could see this in the way they went for the water. At this precise moment Nalghati Female moved in efficiently for the kill.

Thus the cubs were well provided for all through the parched summer months. The male cub, Ashoka, was quite bold, but his sister, Nalghati Beti, remained shy. He dominated her and at kills invariably ate first. He had the advantage of size, weight and strength. Kublai, their father, seemed to be keeping in regular touch. Sightings were rare but he left his pug-marks all over the place.

Learning to Hunt

In October, the park re-opened after the monsoons. The tiger family was ranging far and wide. Water was scattered so that prey movements were not predictable. Fortunately, the cubs had grown used to travelling long distances. As winter approached tiger sightings became more irregular. But with the passing of winter, the prey animals began to be drawn, once again, to the waterholes and the tigers duly followed.

By March, when the cubs were about 15 months old, Nalghati Female had moved the centre of her activity to Phutokot, some distance from Nalghati Valley proper. Here she continued to dispatch deer after deer with cool professionalism. The cubs, too, began to develop their hunting skills. They started catching small prey, such as hares and birds, often helped by luck and as they settled down to hunt with serious intent, it became apparent that both the cubs were equally successful in their endeavours. There is an interesting contrast between male lions and male tigers. Male lions, that take over a pride, live on kills made by pride lionesses during their tenure. Whenever the opportunity arises, a male tiger will also poach kills from the female. Such opportunities occur more frequently whenever a tigress is restricted to a small area, either when she has cubs or when the weather is hot and water is scarce. At these times a male tiger can contact an anchored tigress more easily and help himself to her kills. However, there are long spells in a year when a male has to find food on his own in order to survive. In similar circumstances, the nomadic male lions of Africa have one advantage, they often scavenge, particularly kills made by hyenas. While spotted hyenas are numerous in Africa, often living in large packs and regularly killing on their own, the solitary striped hyena of Ranthambhore is a rarity. A male tiger in Ranthambhore cannot rely on scavenging kills made by a hyena or, for that matter, a leopard.

The Family Splits

Ashoka appeared as proficient as his sister at hunting small prey. He was quite active and, in fact, tried harder than his sister. The cubs also often tried to hunt in tandem - with mixed success. They would approach the intended victim from different directions and inevitably one of them would spook the prey animal, hopefully into the other's path. This co-operative hunting was probably largely instinctive. Ashoka apparently took the initiative in such ventures and he was the first to successfully complete a hunting movement entirely on his own. Once he had tasted the achievement of being able to hunt solo, he began to be drawn towards a solitary lifestyle. The separation process was slow and protracted, however, and even as late as June 1987, when the cubs were 28 months old, they were in regular contact.

A distinctive change occurred with the 87/88 viewing season which began in October. Nalghati Female was rarely seen in Nalghati Valley and she eventually left the valley altogether. She was pregnant again and probably wanted seclusion from her sub-adult young. In May 1988, she was seen some distance away with three new cubs. The queen of Nalghati Valley for five years had finally abdicated.

Meanwhile Ashoka was definitely on his way to independence. Like all young males, he appeared preoccupied with exploring new areas with a view to establishing his own turf elsewhere. The footloose male separated from his sister sometime in mid-1988. It is difficult to be more precise about the date, their contact became increasingly irregular and finally ceased altogether. Although the two became independent, they were destined to form a new alliance two years later. In the meantime, Nalghati Beti showed no obvious inclination to move out of the valley. She seemed likely to continue the dynastic occupation of the area.

As Ashoka searched for his own home range, Kublai, his father, tolerated him, but only just. In fact, with the gradual withdrawal of Nalghati Female, Kublai had taken to spending more time at Noon's dinner table next door at the lakes. Later on in this book we shall be following the fortunes of many tigers, including Noon, but the shadowy figure of Ashoka will always loom somewhere in the background.

Daku, the resident male of the Bakola-Lakarda area. Daku - so-called because he made it a habit of poaching kills executed by Laxmi and Bakola Ben - was a huge male and epitomised the power of the world's biggest land predator, the tiger. Not a big cat to mess around with.

Queen Noon

NOON, THE RESIDENT TIGRESS OF THE LAKES, STARTS A FAMILY

As usual on an April dawn, Padam lake was beautifully lit and vibrating with activity. Expectations of an eventful morning were raised and, for once, such expectations were justified. First we spotted the tigress Noon behind a bush. Then, as she moved through the tall grass bordering the lake, two playful cubs followed. The eleven month old cubs were in energetic mood, investigating anything remotely interesting. The family then slipped into tall grass again and appeared to be heading for a clearing where chital often gather to graze. Chital can't resist the succulent green shoots that sprout here and not surprisingly, Noon always surveyed this grazing meadow whenever she was looking for prey.

The two cubs positioned themselves in the tall grass bordering the meadow and then charged at the chital. They couldn't possibly have hoped to catch the animals ahead of them for the separating distance was great and chital are nimble on their feet, but the panic stricken deer scattered in all directions and Noon almost caught one. She had been lying concealed, anticipating a stray chital blundering into her. Only inches had separated her lunging forelimbs from the rump of the chital doe. Although it was the narrowest of misses, Noon betrayed no emotion as she proceeded to groom herself. The male cub found her and hurled himself at her with great joy. Mother and son played a little and then settled down.

The female cub (call her Noorjahan for she was incredibly pretty), had continued her charge for a longish distance, determined to gain ground on the escaping deer. She had to give up, though, as the distance separating them refused to narrow. A few minutes after stopping, she realised that she was quite alone, cut off from the others, so like a baby, she sat down and started calling. Her appeal changed to a fierce snarl when she spotted us watching her. She began to retrace her steps and almost immediately, she bumped into her brother, apparently searching for her. In typical youthful fashion, the two celebrated the reunion by climbing up a tall tree, expending considerable energy in the process.

Tigers and Other Animals

Noon, the sister of Nalghati Female, became the resident tigress of the lakes eco-system sometime during 1983. At that time, there was an interesting male tiger, called Gengis, occupying the lakes. Gengis' speciality was catching sambar deer in the water. A congregation of sambar in water is quite unusual since they are normally shy and elusive and disperse into the forest. But as the temperature rises and water becomes scarce, the sambar become drawn to the lakes. They take the opportunity to wade into the water and feed on water plants. They quite revel in this even though it is a risky business. Danger to the sambar comes from two unrelated sources. Once, we heard a sambar calling plaintively. A few minutes later, upon following the vocal lead, we noticed agitation in the water directly beneath Rajbagh Palace. Every few minutes, the water surface would be broken by crocodiles, lunging, rolling and twisting. Then a sambar's leg stuck out. The attacked deer must have been feeding on water weeds earlier and had probably become too engrossed, presenting an opportunity to a crocodile to creep up and pull it in. Other crocodiles in the lake must have then joined in the feast, twisting and turning to break up the carcass into manageable chunks.

While sambar fawns do fall victim to the 100-plus marsh crocodiles at Ranthambore, the stronger and more experienced adult sambar usually cope competently with marauding crocodiles. But in late 1983 and early 1984 even they were seriously threatened: Gengis was busy hunting. He had worked out a hunting strategy for catching sambar feeding on the lakes' water plants.

Noon's two cubs charge at a herd of grazing Chital. Noon, herself, was lying concealed in tall grass, ready to pounce on stray chital running her way. One did but Noon missed by inches.

A Sambar hind grazes on weeds at the edge of Rajbagh Lake. The Sambar around the lakes regularly feed on aquatic plants.

Wild boar feeding in the shallow waters of Rajbagh Lake. They are also often seen wallowing in the mud at the water's edge. It is an activity which apparently imparts great delight.

Noon was an interested spectator at some of these water hunts and when Gengis disappeared, she, too, took to hunting the sambar in water.

Noon, like Gengis, was also versatile. A good reason for this is the wide variety of prey that frequents the lakes. There were the sambar, of course, and there were the chital. Unlike the sambar, chital avoid going into water but they love to feed on the grass that sprouts up as the shallow lakes dry out at the edges. It is a common sight to see sambar braving the water in search of aquatic weeds with chital grazing on the damp shoreline. Although chital are quite quick on their feet, Noon caught them regularly. This was partly because chital were around in considerable numbers and partly due to the fact that Noon became quite an expert operator in the generally open terrain of the lakes, making skilful use of the remnants of cover.

Like the chital, wild boar love to busy themselves on the lake shores. But unlike the chital, they sometimes wade into the lake waters to dig out the water plants. In contrast to the sambar, they stay in the shallows. Most wild boars in Ranthambore are quite mobile, moving purposefully in small groups. They also have a tendency to run through the tall grass fringing the lakes and this occasionally serves to disrupt the peaceful grazing of the deer; from a distance a wild boar can be mistaken for a predator and its rapid gait arouses suspicion. The more nervous deer call out, causing others to join in. Panic spreads and the herd may stampede. In recent years the wild boar population has grown with a concurrent increase in false deer alarm calls.

Noon Vanishes

Noon's association with the lakes and her hunting in the relatively open terrain made her highly visible and hence famous with visitors. She was impassive and tolerant, taking fame and adulation in her stride. She thrilled visitors right up to the end of April 1986 and then she vanished.

An egret using a sambar stag's back as a fishing perch. Sambars in Ranthambhore regularly wade into the picturesque lakes to feed on the aquatic vegetation. Egrets take the opportunity to catch something edible, made visible by the sambars' stirring up of the water

The reason for Noon's disappearance was discovered in early June when a small gang of road workers stumbled upon tiger cubs in a thick bush some distance from a ravine. They had intended to 'go behind a bush' but had returned prematurely, scampering desperately up the slope. This ravine, next to the main road into the park, has a perpetual supply of water, is densely vegetated, and is connected by a nala to Padam lake. Although the two cubs were in a very secure den in a thick green bush surrounded by bamboo, Noon moved them nearer the lakes a few days later. Perhaps she had sensed that humans were keeping a benign eye on the den in the ravine and had reacted. In fact she moved the cubs several times more until the monsoon rains descended in early July. Hardly anyone had the chance to catch even a glimpse of her litter.

Wildlife at the Lakes

The cubs were a male-female pair. The lakes must have been bewildering to them at first, but gradually the surrounding area became one great adventure playground. There is always something fascinating to watch or chase at the lakes. The tiny cubs watched the large mammals with awe but relished pursuing the small fry, the birds in particular. The lakes are an excellent place to view the resident and the migratory water birds. There are the omnipresent herons and egrets and a sprinkling of ibises. Cormorants and darters can be seen fishing and drying their wings alongside painted, black, and white-necked storks. There are various types of geese, ducks and dabchicks floating serenely on the water surface but it is the waders, the stilts and the lapwings that the cubs found irresistible since they could be rushed at on land and appeared deceptively easy to catch.

It is the bird often identified with India, the peafowl, however, which provided the cubs with practice. Peafowl are plentiful in Ranthambore. The male, the peacock, is seen either alone or in attendance to several peahens. In the spring he displays his feathers to the peahen, rotating slowly in a full or semi-circle, quivering his body at the same time. Although he goes through this spectacular display in all seriousness, the peahens appear not to take the slightest bit of notice. In winter, a peahen is usually accompanied by her young and they are irresistible to excited tiger cubs. Eventually, after numerous attempts, a cub manages to catch these birds. Success is partly due to the high density of peafowl and partly because they appear to be rather careless birds.

Indian hares are also commonly found at the lakes and the energetic cubs found them irresistible as well. The hare is a tempting target because it often sits still, begging to be stalked. At the last minute, however, it breaks out into a frenzied run, providing the enticed cubs with a thrilling pursuit. The cubs appeared to gain courage whenever an animal ran away from them. Occasionally, however, an animal did not, leaving them perplexed. Once Noorjahan spotted a sounder of wild boar trotting along the lake and she was swift to follow them. She gained ground on the young ones but the sow slowed and then whirled around, to calmly face the oncoming tigress. Noorjahan braked, and then appeared nonplussed when the sow refused to give ground. With Noorjahan remaining indecisive, the sow smirked and then trotted away, looking thoroughly satisfied. Noorjahan tried to save face by concentrating hard on cleaning herself, licking her forepaws and tugging at one or two apparently critical spots on her fur.

In the spring, the peacock displays his feathers to the peahens, slowly rotating in full or semi-circles, quivering his body at the same time. The idea is to signal his fitness and thereby be selected by a peahen.

The Growing Cubs

By the time the cubs were six months old, it became clear that Noorjahan was the submissive cub. This became apparent when food was scarce. When, in late November, Noon crept upon a new born chital fawn and pinned it down, the

Noorjahan stalking an Indian moorhen on a grass-fringed shore of Padam Lake. The tiger cubs found wading birds most attractive to stalk since they could be pursued on land and appeared deceptively easy to catch.

Being fond of water plants, adult Sambar deer often venture deep into the lakes. It is hazardous since marsh crocodiles lurk here, so that any hint of danger causes the Sambar to flee.

male cub snatched the kill away and emphatically refused to share it. This domination hastened the growth of the male cub and of his confidence, so that Noorjahan was drawn to Noon for consolation and reassurance.

Domination apart, the two cubs were very close. One reason for this was that Noon often left them on their own while she searched for prey or went on territorial patrol. She, like all tigresses, had no qualms about leaving her cubs alone for a long period. Tigers are like that, they have this admirable capacity to blend with the rhythm of natural time. Thus Noon would often fall asleep waiting in ambush. Upon waking, she would leisurely make her way to the next hunting spot, marking on the way, grooming herself at a convenient place, always in tune with her immediate environment. The cubs would sometimes be on their own for up to two days.

Left on their own, brother and sister would sleep most of the time. But when awake, they were well aware of her absence and often sat expectantly, anticipating her return. Whenever Noon came back with the intention of leading the cubs to a kill, she hardly got a moment's peace. Nuzzling her and catching the smell of meat, they would become visibly excited and try to cajole their mother into leading them to the carcass straight away. But Noon would characteristically take her time. She would even lie down to toy with her cubs, stretching out, pawing them and giving gentle, affectionate bites. All this would drive the cubs to a hysterical state and eventually she would relent and lead them, meandering, to the kill.

In January, when the cubs were about nine months old, they took a significant step towards adulthood. One day, when the three were walking openly on a dirt track, the cubs ahead and Noon some distance behind, the young ones were seen by a sambar in the adjoining forest and it called out. Noon must have instantly worked out that the sambar was sandwiched between the cubs and herself. She anticipated the spot at which the deer would emerge and positioned herself behind a rock. The plan worked as she charged at the right moment and killed the large hind just a few meters from the track. The cubs' role had been unintentional, but its significance was not lost on them. From then on the family developed the technique of co-operative hunting.

From March to June, as the warmth of spring turned to the heat of summer, the cubs were active at dawn and dusk. During the daytime, they just lazed around. The duo were now quite fearless of other wildlife, although whenever

A magnificent Sambar stag staring at a slight movement in the thicket in front of him.

they waded into the lakes, they put on a snarling ritual for the benefit of real and imaginary crocodiles. As for people in vehicles, they were viewed simply as part of the scenery. As a result, it was sometimes possible to see the cubs during the day, lazing by the lakeshore or in some shaded pool of water. Like adult tigers, they sought cover to escape the heat, but unlike adults, they did not bother to hide completely.

The Tiger's Day

So life was good. One typical day went like this: At dawn we found Noon and the cubs sitting in the middle of a dirt track. They had obviously just finished feeding on a kill, hidden in the tall grass, and had emerged to catch the first rays of the sun. After a few minutes, something stirred near the kill and presently Kublai appeared. The three tigers on the track did not visibly acknowledge his appearance, perhaps indicating their familiarity with the huge male. For his part, the well-fed Kublai was in no mood for ceremony. Giving the trio a cursory glance, he climbed up a hill and, walking briskly, disappeared from sight. There had been no nuzzling, no fond goodbye, it was all very matter of fact.

Within fifteen minutes, Noon and her cubs were also on the move, slowly making their way to a favourite resting spot in Jalra forest, next to Padam lake. The male cub led, Noorjahan keeping Noon company. Occasionally, Noon would lovingly bite her daughter's ear - the two were very close. In Jalra forest, Noon left the cubs and lay in the tall grass fringing the lake. This patch is shaded by a large tree and a cool breeze sweeps up from the lake.

The sounds of the forest were subdued until about five when sudden langur alarm calls led us to Noorjahan sitting in a small pool in Jalra. After a longish lie-in she stepped out, her coat plastered in mud from below. She shook her paws, gingerly, and then climbed up a rocky incline, the low angle of the sun highlighting her wet silhouette. She then looked for Noon, of course. It took her a while to find her mother who was hidden in tall grass (tigers have only a moderately good sense of smell). In due course, Noorjahan's brother joined them and the family slept together. No one, without prior information, could have guessed their whereabouts. It was a tranquil scene soaked through by the evening sun, and it was only the knowledge of the hidden tigers that lent the landscape a touch of excitement

True to form, Noon emerged at dusk to sit in the open. She seemed to be surveying her wild domain with great satisfaction, but whatever her thoughts, her cubs arrived to interrupt them. The family exchanged some affectionate greetings, the cubs behaving as if they had missed Noon's short absence a great deal. She seemed deeply contented as the cubs frolicked around her and when they joined her for a family portrait, she expressed profound pride. But this glimpse into their domestic life was soon over for as the sun gave up the unequal struggle to keep above the horizon, the tigers stirred into action. Noon moved purposefully and the cubs followed. As they disappeared, swallowed into the darkening shadows, the question kept coming back: what do tigers really get up to at night? Honestly, we really don't know.

The weak monsoons came and went but Noon and her cubs stayed on. October of 1987 found the family operating around Malik lake. The cubs were now seventeen months old, on the threshold of independence, although still catching small prey on their own. However, Noon was making sure that they did not go hungry.

Noorjahan climbs up a rocky incline. After a longish soak in a small pool, the little tigress stepped out, her coat plastered in mud from below. She gingerly shook her paws, one by one, and then moved on to look for her mother, Noon.

Noon sits for a family portrait. The cubs are approximately eleven months old and about half the size of their mother on whom they are totally dependent for survival.

The Cubs Mature

Imperceptibly but inevitably, the separation process began. Noon spent more time on her own. The cubs, instead of yearning for Noon's return, kept themselves busy. Noon had done an excellent job in familiarising them with her home range and the cubs moved about at ease. But they still moved together. Even while resting, they kept in visual contact. Perhaps companionship provided the young cubs with security and confidence.

In the new year the male cub's instinct for a solitary lifestyle began to draw him away on his own. As winter passed into spring, the pull grew stronger. He experimented with hunting at the lakes by charging into the water in hot pursuit of startled sambar. However, his success rate was dismal. Noorjahan, for her part, tried to keep up with him. But she also remained in close contact with Noon. It was as if, in comparison with her intrepid brother, she was timid and needed her mother's presence to boost her confidence.

One day in early March, Noon and her cubs had come together on a kill, and by the time feeding had stopped in the evening, the replete tigers could hardly move. However, early next morning, perhaps responding to an urge to exercise, the tigers left the kill site together and proceeded leisurely along the grass-fringed shore. Noon spotted a chital fawn and, despite being heavy with food, she gave in to her instinct to hunt. She caught the fawn but instead of killing it, she presented it live to the cubs. They gleefully accepted it, slapping it with their paws and repeatedly tripping it up. After a few minutes, one of them could not resist the urge to bite through the fawn's neck. Then a game ensued in which one of the two carried the dangling fawn in its jaws, the other running alongside to snatch it away. They soon tired of this and moved on, leaving the uneaten fawn behind. A cheetah mother regularly brings live prey to release it for their cubs to practise on. But in Noon's case, this appears to have been a chance event.

During spring, the three tigers were seen together only on kills. The male cub was heading decisively toward a solitary lifestyle. Consequently, Noorjahan found herself increasingly on her own. She was active though, spending quite some time stalking animals that she had little chance of catching. Her stalks were always sensuous and bewitching as her elastic body effortlessly contorted to glide through cover. But although her body control was skilful, her judgment was tarnished with impatience. She had yet to learn that charging over 30 meters in open terrain at alerted chital is quite unproductive.

Nilgai Kill

This didn't matter, for there was still Noon. In late April we found the family finishing off a nilgai kill at the Mori waterhole which is sandwiched between Padam and Rajbagh lakes. Nilgai is the largest antelope native to Asia. It looks ungainly, but is quite speedy. It is obviously not an easy animal to hunt but a tiger with Noon's cunning and expertise will not hesitate to tackle even a 250 kg male nilgai should a good opportunity arise. Female nilgai with calves are the more frequent targets of tiger attacks. In 1988 there were over a thousand nilgai scattered over the more open areas of Ranthambore.

Noon and the male cub were at the water-hole, Noorjahan a little distance away. There was probably a little tension amongst them for when Noorjahan approached the duo, both mother and son gave warning growls. Noorjahan stood indecisively and then sat down. After a while, her brother got up and moved twenty metres away before slipping into the water, his body fringed by green water plants. Thereupon, Noorjahan sauntered up to Noon and arranged herself next to her mother. As the afternoon gave way to evening, the male cub got out of water and padded out of view. Noon, too, walked away, followed by Noorjahan who first dragged the remnants of the kill into tall grass.

Separate Ways

The three tigers were seen together for the last time in mid-May, 1988. The cubs were then two years old and managing on their own for long periods. As the male cub was ranging further and further afield, driven by that mysterious urge to strike out for his own dominion, Noorjahan was at ease at the lakes, within calling distance of Noon. Kublai was very much around, although preferring to lurk in the background. He did emerge from the shadows once though, having a soak at a waterhole, in the company of Noorjahan, in the blistering heat of May.

That's how the lakes' tigers were at the closing of the tiger-viewing season - Kublai, the undisputed master, watching over Noon and Noorjahan, with the male cub about to sever the paternal cord.

Noorjahan, Noon's adolescent female cub, has spotted grazing chital deer in the distance and commenced on a long stalk. This is an example of how the coat colour and pattern of the tiger can blend with its surroundings. Good camouflage often helps a tiger to get within striking distance of its prey.

Enter Bhaiyu

FAMILY LIFE IN SEMLI WITH LAXMI AND HER CUBS – BHAIYU, CHOTI AND BELA

It wasn't a comfortable morning to be outdoors; the sky was cloudless, the sun was shining fiercely, a hat offered little protection and the nearest shady tree was fifty metres away. But the three tigers more than made up for the discomfort. They were siblings, about 14 months old, and all three were lying in a pool with only their heads above the water. They seemed to have surrendered to lethargy. Now was our opportunity to study their faces and revise their facial markings for future reference. For at maturity, they were bound to separate and probably disappear from human gaze, but if they reappeared, we could identify them. In the meantime, the trio were close together both mentally and physically. Their mother, though, had slipped quietly away on some project of her own.

Laxmi

She was Laxmi, the only female in a litter of five born to the tigress Padmini in 1976. All had survived to maturity. Laxmi had struck out on her own in late 1978 and had become a mother herself in 1982. Padmini was still around and in 1981 she had Noon, Nalghati Female and their brother. Padmini herself disappeared in 1983 and consequently the focus shifted to Nalghati Female, Noon and their elder sister, Laxmi. Encounters between the three were infrequent so it is unlikely that Laxmi related herself to Noon and Nalghati Female in any special way. The reason for infrequent encounters is the system of home ranges that the tigers have and in that system rights are respected. Next to Nalghati Female's home range of Nalghati Valley were Noon's lakes. The main track continues past the lakes and after 7 kilometres arrives at the ruins of Lakarda village, centre of Laxmi's home range. The track then continues through rather monotonous landscape for several kilometres to a right turning for Semli valley. Tiny and picturesque, if there is a heaven for tiger cubs then Semli valley must be it. The valley is just within Laxmi's home range and beyond it lies Bakola, the home range of another fascinating tiger whom we shall be meeting in the next chapter.

The New Arrivals

Semli valley is usually green, thanks to an underground stream entering from the Lakarda side, which flows towards Bakola. The small valley floods in the Monsoons, and the valley sides sprout lush green grass which chital find irresistible. These deer,with dotted coats and dainty ways, give the valley a fairy tale atmosphere. There is also a nala which connects Semli with the area of Bakola and is frequently used by tigers. At the mouth of the nala, almost inside Semli valley, there are a number of caves.Laxmi gave birth to her cubs here, sometime in January, 1986.

The cubs were first seen in March by a Swiss photographer. He nearly fell out of his jeep when a two month old cub crossed the track in front of him. He reported the sighting to the park management who promptly ordered all drivers to keep out of Semli, a sensible order if only the park vehicles had done the same. Instead, the management vehicles took advantage of this monopoly in viewing rights and converged gleefully on Semli daily. The viewing was good but intermittent since the tolerant Laxmi often took off with her brood, disappearing from view whenever she chose to.

Genes and Nutrients

The male cub was named Bhaiyu, and the two females, Bela and Choti. Bhaiyu - a word of endearment - is Hindi for 'brother'. From the start Bhaiyu dominated the scene. He was he the largest of the trio, and he also appeared to get the better of Laxmi, perhaps he sensed that she had a weakness for him.

Having fed, Laxmi's two adolescent daughters, Bela on the left and Choti on the right, enjoy a lie-in. Note that their entire bodies, save for the heads, are immersed in water. It has been repeatedly observed that tigers do not like getting their faces wet.

Male cubs grow more rapidly than females, probably due to a combination of genes and nourishment. Males are programmed to grow bigger : the initial advantage of size lying in their genes. In addition, males receive better nourishment starting from day one, obtaining a bigger share of the food provided by the mother. Do tiger mothers favour their sons? Take Bhaiyu, for example. It was usually the case that whenever Laxmi killed a small animal, Bhaiyu would snatch the kill away from Laxmi and eat it all by himself, growling intermittently. Laxmi and the other two would wait nearby until Bhaiyu was ready to share. He would signal this by ceasing growling, visibly relaxing, and ignoring the first of the approaching females.

Why is a tigress biased towards sons? The answer rests on the assumption that a tigress wants the maximum number of grandchildren. This reflects an instinct for the survival of her own kind. The reasoning is that a healthy tigress, such as Laxmi, wants healthy male cubs, such as Bhaiyu, since males have the potential to sire more offspring than comparatively healthy daughters can produce. So should the well-nourished and fast growing Bhaiyu turn out to be bigger and stronger than the average male, he wins in the competition for tigresses, and fathers an above average number of offspring, thus providing Laxmi with a large number of grandchildren.

Bhaiyu and Humans

Bhaiyu looked set to dominate the scene. He bullied his sisters and Laxmi let him have his own way. He became confident, even audacious, in the almost danger-free environment. At this time Ranthambhore was well protected from human intrusions. Although there were sloth bears around, an encounter in Semli between a growing tiger and an adult sloth bear was highly unlikely. So Bhaiyu had the run of Semli.

Bhaiyu also developed his curiousity, being keenly aware of his surroundings. Movement fascinated him most and even as he rested, his eyes closely followed motion. Once he was sitting alone, regal style, on a rock ledge, calmly surveying a few jeeps whose occupants were delighted at having an alert young tiger in full view. Then one occupant decided to change jeeps perhaps to obtain a different view of Bhaiyu, and so got down and started walking. Everyone else present ceased murmuring. Bhaiyu stiffened. His unblinking eyes followed the foolhardy man, his paws twitched and he lowered his head. Then his tail flicked and his rump wriggled, a sure signal that he was about to attack. Just then, the man boarded a jeep and Bhaiyu relaxed as did everyone else. No one reprimanded the culprit, for he was a VIP with power to punish anyone who would have dared. But the silence that engulfed him and the looks he got from his companions spoke volumes. He must have felt very small indeed.

Bhaiyu did let fly one day. He was by a dirt track when a jeepload of park officials whizzed past.Covered in dust, he looked askance at the fast-disappearing vehicle. The dust settled, and he once again rested his chin on his forepaws and closed his eyes. However, his siesta was again interrupted as the sound of a distant diesel-engine signalled the jeep's return. Bhaiyu's eyes narrowed and he lowered his head. As the jeep approached, he flattened his ears backwards and flicked his tail from side to side. The jeep appeared and Bhaiyu leapt out. But he had miscalculated the speed of the vehicle and missed. Still, he bounded after it. Although the driver was not aware of the hurtling feline missile as he was driving at speed, the passengers in the open rear were terrified and screamed in fear. Much to their obvious relief, and Bhaiyu's regret, the jeep remained outside the young tiger's grasp.

Choti

Choti, the smallest of the three cubs, was not afraid to approach vehicles either, but she preferred stationary ones. Choti had the added ingredient of friendliness. She would approach close, look to check, and if satisfied, sit down and even curl up to to sleep within a few metres of the jeep. For a friendly little tigress, the name of Choti, a term of affection in Hindi for someone small was quite apt.

Choti also loved resting on low tree branches. At about 4.00 p.m. one afternoon we found her resting in a shady spot in Semli. She moved to sit in a tiny pool, one of the few remnants of the area's rapidly drying stream. At about 6.00 p.m. Bela appeared, whereupon Choti got up, apparently to greet her sister. But halfway she changed direction and made for a palm tree where she raked her claws on the trunk, stretching her body at the same time. Her exercise over, she walked straight at us. She circled the jeep, then heaved herself up the nearby dead tree and settled down, one metre above our heads, her paws dangling, her eyes upon us, and a serene expression on her face. We could have reached out and stroked her whiskers. There was no trepidation on either side, neither was there a bond between her and us. We were just a peculiar feature of the environment as far as she was concerned.Then, as if to demonstrate the limits of peaceful co-existence, she slipped down the tree and disappeared into the forest of the valley without a single backward look. She had returned to prowl her world.

Petit Choti rakes her claws on the trunk of a palm tree in Semli Valley. She held the extended posture, front feet on the trunk and hind legs on the ground, for about 30 seconds.

Choti resting on a dead tree, wearing a serene expression on her face. Tree-climbing doesn't come easily but the lighter tiger cubs manage better than the heavier adults.

Conventional reasons given for African lions climbing trees are that up there they catch a breeze and so keep cool; it is a refuge from tormenting flies; and it is a vantage point from which to spot prey. In Choti's case, the last two reasons are not really applicable since flies are not a menace in Ranthambhore and she depended on Laxmi for food. The first explanation also has little plausibility since she never stayed for long on a tree. The most plausible reason is that like all the young tigers of Ranthambhore, the Semli trio played around and on trees a lot. Choti, the lightest in weight and the most agile, probably had the better of the other two when play involved trees so she utilized her advantage to the full and got into the habit of tree-climbing. As the cubs put on weight, Bela and Bhaiyu grew out of tree-climbing but Choti continued the habit for some time.

Choti was the closest of the three to Laxmi. She was the first to run up and greet her mother returning from a hunt. Whenever Bhaiyu took possession of a kill, Choti invariably sought solace from Laxmi. It wasn't that Laxmi was less fond of Bhaiyu or Bela, it was just the way pairing occurred in that tiger quartet. Bela was somewhat mysterious. She was difficult to observe,was disinterested in vehicles and their occupants, and inclined to relax amidst foliage. Like most shadowy personalities, she was to spring a surprise a few years later.

This sharp-eyed Langur monkey atop a flowering 'Flame of the Forest' tree will bark out alarm calls should it spot a tiger.

The Cubs Learn

Sheltered in the compact, romantic valley, with Laxmi around to provide food and comfort, the cubs grew fast. They were usually eager and alert, ready to chase moving animals. Sometimes their bluff was called, like when a big male wild boar refused to be chased, and occasionally they were chased in turn, like when a sloth bear with a short temper took offence at their insouciance. They were ready to chase at anytime. Once, in the 45°C heat of the afternoon, Bhaiyu, panting heavily in shade, saw a hare and had a go at full speed without second thoughts.

Gradually, however, the cubs became more discriminating in their selection and timing. Learning to discriminate in this way is a distinct phase in a young cub's life when they learn to ration their energy. The cub realises that catching requires more skills than wild chasing. A matter of fact tigress, Laxmi taught her cubs the finer points of hunting by unplanned example, taking the teaching of cubs literally in her stride whenever she took them on walkabouts. So while she went about the daily task of living, the cubs played, explored, watched her hunt, absorbed the information and processed it. The processing cannot be too difficult since cubs have in place hunting instincts to build upon. The finer points - tripping or over-balancing a running prey animal, applying a neck or throat bite - are more difficult and are acquired by trial and error.

Another interesting development was illustrated late one evening when the three were sitting apart to form a semi-circle into which walked a civet. Bhaiyu, the nearest, watched the civet closely, his rump quivering with excitement. The temptation proved overpowering and he let fly a fraction too early. But the other two had been fascinated spectators too, and as the civet flew past, Bela pounced and missed. The civet somehow escaped a charging Choti and then managed to shoot up a tree pursued by the excited trio. But far from having a miraculous escape, the troubles of the tiny carnivore were just beginning. The big cats must have kept a vigil throughout the night for the next morning we found the civet, still in the tree above and the three tigers down below. Oddly enough, the hapless civet was being harassed by crows that were diving into the tree and crowing raucously. At about six p.m. we discovered it lying lifelessly on the ground, wet and uneaten.

Bela attempting to drag a sambar carcass into cover. Pulling it in the shady, luxuriant kill-site, the kill got trapped between heavy branches lying on the forest floor. Bela's reaction was to tighten her grip and pull hard, arching her body and using her forelimbs in support. It was slow work.

A Remarkable Hunt

This incident was illuminating in that it showed that the trio could react quickly and co-ordinate instinctively. This behaviour was reinforced when we witnessed a remarkable hunt that took place in the fading light. The three cubs were lying in ambush near Semli's shrunken stream. On the opposite side, hesitant sambar appeared to be assessing the risks of a strike to the stream for a quick drink. Unknown to them , Laxmi had slipped into position in the forest behind them. As the heat took its toll, the deer gave in to the temptation and started the descent to the rivulet. Fear still exerted a weak pull though, for the lead sambar would occasionally stop to tentatively raise a foreleg, in readiness to stamp it on the ground. But thirst clouded its judgment and it failed to pick out the feline trio. So it was too late when, upon seeing three pairs of gleaming eyes, it spun round and ran, panicking the rest of the herd. The three tigers burst out from the sparse cover and chasing hard, managed to drive one sambar in the general direction of Laxmi. When the sambar was in range, Laxmi broke cover and after a noisy short chase in the forest, completed her task.

It was a king vulture that gave the tigers away the next morning. It was sitting on a branch, busily cleaning its beak. After a little searching, we located the kill at the mouth of the nala that links Semli Valley to Bakola. The carcass was fragmented, four hungry tigers had seen to that. Bhaiyu was working on the biggest piece of bone, scraping the remnants of the flesh with his rough tongue. Although engrossed, he still sent hostile vibes to his sisters. Perceiving that he was in no mood for sharing, Bela sniffed around, hoping for scraps. Finding none, she nuzzled Choti and settled down for a soak. But Choti walked a few paces through the dark water, lowered her face, and lifted out a small piece of the kill.With her bounty clasped in her jaws, she checked her surroundings. Satisfied, she settled down to a session of leisurely nibbling. Meanwhile Laxmi, feeling the rising morning heat, had slipped quietly into the pool. She soaked herself with one paw, in characteristic tiger fashion, holding the side of the waterhole. it was odd to think how the family was spaced out and yet together.

Laxmi's twin sister cubs, Bela and Choti, nuzzle in a water-hole.

A standing Choti yawns one more time before moving off to resume her search for prey. Smallest in size of the Semli triplets borne by Laxmi, Choti was the least bothered by vehicles. At times she would fall asleep within a few meters of a stationary jeep.

The four tigers were seen to hunt co-operatively several times. The basic plan was for the youngsters to drive the prey into the path of their concealed mother. The cubs were imprecise in this and usually managed to create bedlam amongst the prey. But the chances of a prey animal dashing in Laxmi's direction were good. There was also a variation in hunting technique when the three cubs would separate, lion style, and approach the grazing prey from different directions. But since none of the cubs could yet hunt on its own, this was a zero return technique.

The quartet were also seen sharing kills with a male tiger who must have been the father. He was a huge animal in his prime and was called Daku. He was a loner really, and even at kills he would feed and sit apart. But the cubs had no fear of Daku and would sometimes nuzzle up to his face. He appeared not to like it, but apart from a grimace of annoyance, he did little else to discourage such sloppy behaviour.

From Cub to Tigress

The monsoon rains of 1987 were poor and patchy but the 87-88 season that began in October had, at least, a superficial freshness about it. Laxmi's cubs were beginning a new phase in their lives, experimenting with separation, but retaining habits from their past. This was delicately sketched out one cold and hazy evening when we encountered Choti all by herself. She was searching for prey, and going about it in a relaxed manner. In fact, after several minutes, she sat down with a deep sigh, groomed herself and watched us with unblinking eyes. Then her yawning commenced, gently impelling her to move, first to stretch herself and scratch a tree, and then to take a better look at us. After a close examination, she yawned and then returned to her task of hunting. As she glided smoothly through the grass and out of sight, it was apparent that the little one had become a tigress. She had serious work to do, all on her own.

A few days later, we encountered Laxmi all alone. She, too, was looking for prey and, like Choti, she appeared to have all the time in the world, some of which she took to have a rest, keeping us in sight. She had no particular interest in us, of course, and in fact none of the tourist vehicles really mattered to her. Laxmi, however, was well-mannered and allowed us to watch her for some time. But inevitably, she commenced the ritual which signalled her intention to move. So she groomed herself, yawned, stretched and then was gone. That's the way it is with adult tigers, their's is a mysterious life that they have to live out.

Bhaiyu investigating a scent. Upon spotting a familiar tree where a tiger might have left olfactory signs, Bhaiyu eagerly walked up and stuck his nose out. In order to extract maximum information,

Bhaiyu wrinkles up his nose and hangs his tongue out. This grimace activates a sensory gland in the roof of a tiger's mouth. Bhaiyu held this expression - known as the flehmen gesture - for about 15 seconds

The Exploratory Phase

As for Bhaiyu, he was in an exploratory phase. He was all over the place, turning up where least expected. Smells fascinated him and he took every opportunity to investigate tree trunks, isolated bushes and prominent rocks where a tiger might have left scent marks. Bhaiyu would walk up eagerly and stick his nose out, inhale and then wrinkle his nose to activate a sensory gland in the roof of his mouth. This flehmen gesture enables tigers to extract the maximum information from an olfactory deposit. We can only guess at the richness of information - what it tells about age, sex, condition etc. of the depositor. Bhaiyu, scent-marked frequently too, though at this stage it may have been fairly indiscriminate and not the serious business of asserting his territorial rights.

Rare Meetings

Bhaiyu was usually encountered either alone or with Bela, an indication that the brother - sister bond is more enduring than the mother-son bond in tigers.The bond between mother and daughter is the most enduring of all and Laxmi kept in touch with her daughters long after the latter had attained independence. There were also occasions when the whole family came together, especially when there was food to be shared. It was quite uncanny how the trio located Laxmi when she had killed something big. Such a convergence occurred one day when Laxmi was on the hunt in no-man's land, between Semli and Bakola,near the largish Berda nala. This is an eerie sort of place for there is usually little sign of life here. But on that particular day a small group of sambar was traversing the nala and Laxmi was at the right place. There was the sound of running hooves followed by a cry and then silence. Judging by the length of the pauses between the short dragging sounds, it appeared that she had brought down an adult. As the sounds were moving away from us, she was clearly taking the kill towards the nala bed. The next morning all four tigers were around the kill, Bhaiyu on the carcass, feeding and snarling at the females. Once Bhaiyu had finished, he was friendly again. Throughout, Laxmi proved very elusive, giving only a couple of glimpses of herself. She slipped away unobtrusively at some stage for, in the evening, only the three siblings emerged from the thicket.

Above. Choti crosses a rivulet in Semli Valley to join up with her twin brother, Bhaiyu, resting on the other side. Tiger siblings like to keep in touch with each other until they can hunt on their own. Companionship affords a sense of security. Left, an awe-inspiring sight in nature: a male tiger displaying outright aggression. Here Bhaiyu, on a kill and under cover, viciously snarls at his tentative sisters, baring his huge canines. It is a clear message to keep away.

The frequency of such get-togethers declined and it was after an interval of three months that we next saw the trio together on a kill. In the morning we found Choti and Semli. Lying camouflaged in shade, she had her eyes fixed on the chital and sambar grazing a hundred meters away. Returning that afternoon, we met Bhaiyu, feeding in the tall grass next to the vehicle track. We waited, and Bela duly appeared. As she tentatively approached Bhaiyu, he growled and snarled in reply. Wisely, Bela kept her distance and rolled over in the grass. But Bhaiyu was edgy and notwithstanding the submissive gesture made by Bela, picked up the carcass and climbed up into the dappled forest above. The kill was a sambar baby, plastered with mud.Perhaps the fawn had been drinking when caught – yet Bhaiyu was not muddy. Neither was Bela, who followed him into the forest above. It must have been Choti who had killed and she herself emerged a few minutes later, the tell-tell mud splattered on her belly. She went straight to the spot where Bhaiyu had been feeding and ate some left-overs. Choti looked thin. She studied our jeep and came closer. Inspection finished, she lay down on the track, upside down, four feet up in the air. After resting totally unconcerned like this for five minutes, she got up to join the others. Waiting below for a couple of hours, we could hear the occasional growl. Then, at around six o'clock, Bhaiyu descended, picking his way nimbly around the large rocks strewn over the forest floor. He went directly to the stream for a long drink. Then he lay down with a heavy sigh and looked around with contentment. When his sisters came down they sat near Bhaiyu. As they consoled themselves by grooming their fur, Bhaiyu put his head down and went to sleep.

Mongoose Hunt

As the days grew hotter, with temperatures racing past 40°c and water evaporating even faster, Bhaiyu became increasingly drawn to the nearby habitat of Bakola. This miniature eco-system has permanent water and the cool shade of jamun trees. He would stretch out next to one of the clear pools,seemingly without a care. He was, at two and a half years, still growing and indulged in active playing and chasing without serious intent. One steamy summer afternoon, Bhaiyu was panting heavily as he lay in the cool jamun shade. An adult tiger would probably have fallen asleep but Bhaiyu's eyes were watchful. A mongoose passed by and he picked it out at once. Excited,he crouched and wriggled, preparing to spring. During a tense waiting of fifteen seconds the mongoose, unaware of the quivering cat, first came closer and then veered away. Bhaiyu got up to follow the mongoose which was busily going its own way. Bhaiyu could hardly contain himself and charged, probably a little early. The shocked mongoose managed to shoot out of his reach and then twist sharply up a rock-strewn incline. Although Bhaiyu had severed permanent attachment with Laxmi, he was still young at heart.

The Dutiful Mother

Laxmi was still in touch with her daughters. At about 6.15 p.m. one evening, when we were driving leisurely back to camp, we heard the unmistakable deep, rich roaring of a tiger, floating over the otherwise silent landscape. As we stopped and waited, the roaring drew inexorably closer. Eventually, Laxmi materialized, roaring and walking rapidly. We followed for about a kilometre or so before hearing an answering roar. Laxmi quickened her pace and the two roars drew closer. All other noises of the forest had ceased. Just as Laxmi reached a clearing, Bela emerged from a thicket opposite. Clearly delighted, they greeted enthusiastically, nuzzled repeatedly, and kept rubbing their bodies even as they walked together. Laxmi and Bela came to the vehicle track and then walked along it together, step matching step. Laxmi was heavy and her whiskers were tinged with red; she had come to fetch her daughter to share in the feast she had hidden away somewhere.

The Successful Mother

As the 87-88 season drew to a close, sightings of Laxmi became infrequent. She withdrew into nalas and ravines. It was only her cubs that had brought her out into the open. That, and her history of habituation, had made the wildlife viewing exceptionally rich. At heart, though, she was a remote tigress with an impenetrable personality. During this episode of tiger-watching, we got the impression that she had this vast reservoir of good manners which overrode her preference for being left alone with her cubs; only her royal breeding prevented her from expressing anything more than cool indifference.

So, in keeping with her character, very little of Laxmi was seen over the next year and a half - just enough to confirm her continual presence in Lakarda. However, she would be back with a surprise in late 1989. In the meantime, she had left three tigers for us humans to marvel at. As a mother, she had undoubtedly succeeded. It sounds far-fetched today, but back then we could set out with high hopes at dawn and in all probability find at least one of the trio. If it was Bhaiyu, sprawled beside a pool with his majestic head on a giant paw, he would yield to opening one eyelid before falling asleep again. After all, tomorrow is just another day for tigers in their land.

Top. Bhaiyu, resting but alert, has spotted an unwary mongoose pass by. He intently watches, wriggles his rump and is all set for action. It is very hot but the young tiger is oblivious to the torrid weather.

Middle. Bhaiyu is up and eagerly tracking his quarry. He still hasn't been noticed and is preparing to charge. Young tigers have an irresistible urge to follow small, moving animals.

Right. Bhaiyu charges but misses as the mongoose runs and then sharply twists up the steep incline, making it difficult for the tiger to follow. Then young at heart, Bhaiyu grew out of such expenditure of energy.

Bakola Ben

A GLIMPSE INTO THE LIFE OF AN INCREDIBLE HUNTRESS

It is the spring of 1988 and very hot indeed. The two consequent years of drought are telling on the Park's landscape. The water-table under the park is going down rapidly, the fall being accentuated by the bore-holes that have sprung up outside the park. Rajbagh Talao is drying up fast and the marsh crocodile (muggers) are feasting on its fish trapped in isolated pools of water. These reptiles will not need to eat for a long time. Padam Talao has retained some water and the deer are congregating there in large numbers. Despite all this, no mammal has yet died as a direct result of the shortage of water. But for how long will Ranthambhore continue to be self-sufficient?

There are regular sightings of Nalghati Female's cubs in Nalghati Valley. They should be just over three years old now and independent of their mother. There is no news of Nalghati Female herself, but the father of the cubs, Kublai, is still around, moodily pacing his territory. He appears to be in command of Nalghati Valley and the Lakes, and Noon is still the queen of the lakes. She is sometimes seen alone and sometimes with her two cubs. So, as Kublai drops in occasionally, especially when food is around, the family is, loosely speaking, still together. But the Semli family of Laxmi and her cubs has separated.

From Bakola, there are reports of a tigress who apparently sits all day long under the shade of Chila trees, overlooking a big nala. Some think she is boring and others, over-confident no doubt, ridicule her 'tameness'. Apparently jeeps have driven within 10 metres of her and not produced any reaction. Enter Bakola Ben.

Tiger Life in Bakola

It was a hot April day. We might have fallen asleep, like the tigress before us, except that she was not really sleeping. True, she was stretched out and her eyes were closed but she was lean and hungry and, consequently, fully alert. As if to emphasize this, she opened her eyes momentarily, looked, and closed them again. A deceptive tigress, she was ready for half-chances.

The tigress was Bakola Ben. Ben is Hindi for "sister". She had a dark coat colour, an expressive face with distinctive markings, and a nicked ear, so that most people could quickly identify her. She had been seen in Bakola since early 1985 but may have been around earlier than that. In early 1988 she was probably 7-8 years old.

Bakola has a perpetual supply of water so that there are lush oases of thick and green vegetation throughout the year. There are also a lot of jamun trees, and in the shade of these dense groves there is plenty of cover. Even in very hot weather, the shade is cool. As one enters Bakola, on one side of an evergreen strip there are short, steep cliffs whereas on the other, there are small hills. The landscape is quite dramatic so that driving a jeep into Bakola, you feel as if you are entering a different world. The jeep track continues past the cliffs and presently comes to the area of the Chila trees. From here one can look down into a wide nala which attracts prey animals whenever water collects in its hollows. Bakola is an almost ideal tiger habitat given that it has water, prey, cover and shade. There are also plenty of suitable places for a den site. Bakola would, in fact, appear incomplete without a tiger and Bakola Ben filled the niche perfectly.

Daku

Bakola Ben's home range was within the territory of a male tiger called Daku - short for dacoit. He was so called because he was a past master at the craft of living off his tigresses' kills. Bright orange and in his prime, this large tiger looked even bigger after he had finished off one of Bakola Ben's kills.

Bakola Ben, the resident tigress of Bakola area, interrupts her afternoon nap to gaze at the camera. She gave the superficial impression of docility but we discovered her powerful and fierce personality in some exciting encounters.

Bakola Ben traverses the miniature Bakola gorge. The tigress looks extremely thin, a consequence of not having eaten anything substantial for six days

On average, tigers are marginally heavier than lions and in both species males are bigger than females. So the male tiger is the heaviest of the big cats. After seeing healthy male lions with their huge manes in the moist grasslands of East Africa, one starts to have doubts. By comparison, the male tiger looks sleeker. Perhaps the luxuriant manes of the lions give them an enhanced appearance of size and weight. However, a look at a gorged Daku quickly dispels doubts.

Daku had been regularly seen in Bakola for a long time and, with no evidence of any other males, he probably had undisputed control of the area. He was much more secretive than Bakola Ben, and like the other adult male tigers of Ranthambhore, avoided vehicles. But now and then, particularly on a hot day, he would show himself. Tigers find heat uncomfortable and during the hot season frequently soak themselves in water. Daku had a weakness for water and he could sometimes be thus 'caught'. Reluctant to leave the luxury of the pool, he would tolerate a vehicle at a distance of 20-30 metres, but any closer, or the sound or sight of another vehicle approaching, and the urge to leave would gain the upper hand. He would heave himself out of the pool without ceremony and wearing a sullen look, pad into cover.

Walking Habits

Daku and Bakola Ben were photographed mating in Bakola in February 1986 and in April we saw Bakola Ben on several occasions, albeit briefly each time. On the first occasion she made a regal entry. There was a crow high up in a tree with a piece of meat in its beak. So we waited. A peacock flew across the narrow end of Bakola, a langur called out in alarm, and the shape of a tiger emerged, walking easily towards us. She eased herself in to a pool of water nearby, entering rump first, keeping her head well clear of the water. (tigers love water but dislike getting their faces wet). She had eaten and wore a contented look of a big, cuddly, innocent pussy cat. After only a few minutes, she got out,shook herself, and continued with her evening walk. She repeated the walk often in subsequent years and, with lethal consequences.

Do tigers walk a lot? Like all big cats , they give the impression of laziness, particularly during a hot day. Unlike dogs who are built for long-distance running, cats are built for short, fast rushes. But in winter and at night, tigers are quite active and range widely. By following footprints left by tigers walking on soft tracks, we found that male tigers sometimes walk for 15 km at night, patrolling their large territories. Females walk a lot too, but not as far and wide as the males, since their home ranges are smaller.

Why do the Ranthambore tigers often walk on dirt tracks? Some people think they 'prefer' it i.e. it is comfortable. Interestingly, the tracks in Ranthambhore were made to coincide with ancient tiger trails so that walking on dirt tracks may just be incidental. However, there could be another reason. A tiger can see very well in the dark, since its eyes have great light gathering capacities. Placed at a disadvantage, the prey animals have to rely on sound to warn them of a tiger's approach. Walking on dirt tracks means that a tiger can walk silently and maintain its advantage of vision.

Another New Mother

Bakola Ben did not conceive after her February mating but she gave birth to two cubs in early 1987. According to zoo observations, the gestation period of a tiger is around 105 days. So Bakola Ben and Daku must have mated late in 1986. In April 1987 we saw three sets of footprints for the first time - those of Bakola Ben and her two cubs. We also observed Bakola Ben by herself, quite often and for lengthy spells. She often rested for long hours during daytime at Chila Oudhi (Oudhi stands for a hunting platform) in the shade of Chila trees overlooking the wide nala. She did not seem to do much. Nevertheless a two-man American television crew filmed her in action: dragging kills at dawn, having her kills poached by Daku, and unsuccessfully leaping to catch an unwary langur monkey in a tree.

Why do tigers rest so much during the day? A partial answer is that tigers are entirely carnivorous and have to hunt to survive. The prey species are usually active at dawn or dusk and occasionally throughout the night. So tigers save energy by co-ordinating their activities with those of their prey, and rest for most of the day. However, if the prey animals are active during daylight hours, the tiger adapts and does the same.

Bakola Ben's teats were prominent and full of milk. But she chose not to show her cubs, who proved elusive right into the monsoons. However, after the abysmal rains, from October onwards, she was sometimes glimpsed with them but observers had insufficient time to determine their sex.

A Setback

In January 1988 Bakola Ben appeared limping badly, minus one cub, and on the verge of death. Something terrible had happened. But what? A few people had heard gunshots the previous day but that was all there was to go on. Growing thinner and weaker, she limped around, looking for hares and fawns for herself and her remaining cub. When resting, she licked her wounds, especially the one on her right front paw, vigorously. Did this antiseptic work? It must have because the tide turned in her favour and she pulled through. But the nightmare experience, whatever it was, left a permanent scar on the cub. It became extremely shy. Even when Bakola Ben encouraged the cub to go with her on walks or sit with her in the open, it would bolt at the slightest disturbance, such as the sound of an approaching jeep, 50-100 metres away.

By March, however, order was returning to their life. One early morning we arrived in Bakola to see Bakola Ben and Daku in the water with a carcass, eating peacefully at either end of the unrecognizable kill. Bakola Ben seemed not to notice us but Daku would frequently cast a baleful eye in our direction. He didn't trust us one inch. For a while it was a tranquil scene. Suddenly, Daku snarled and grimaced at Bakola Ben, his ears laid well back. The sounds he made sent shivers down our spines. Obediently, Bakola Ben slipped away and simultaneously something small bolted and made for the hills - it was the cub who had slipped into hiding upon our arrival. Daku continued to feed alone but at the sound of an approaching jeep, he dragged the kill out of the water and took it under a dense bush.

Huntress's Life

The tiger is the ultimate predator. Entirely carnivorous, its body is built to hunt. Since the tiger has prospered whenever it has been shielded from human disturbance, it has to be an efficient hunter. Reading the literature on tiger hunting one can be led to believe that it is a solitary hunter that hunts in a classical manner - a patient stalk, a short charge, catch and bite. But ever since watching Noon and her cubs, and Laxmi's family hunting co-operatively, we were intrigued about the range of a tiger's hunting technique. Moreover, what we had observed on leopard hunting had led us to doubt the implied rigidity of a big cat's hunting behaviour. Being opportunistic and also persistent, leopards are masters of improvisation. They have to be. They do not have the speed of the cheetah or the co-operation of the lion pride. Leopards are cunning hunters. Tigers, too, it seemed need to use opportunity combined with intelligence.

We were able to observe Bakola Ben every day for 35 days from 26th March to 29th April, 1988. Most of the time Bakola Ben was seen alone and either resting or walking - indeed, the image of a tedious tigress. But these periods were interspersed with a considerable variety of other activities, brief but explosive. Beneath Bakola Ben's benign exterior lurked a deadly menace.

Bakola Ben was a versatile huntress and could call upon at least one of the following techniques.

Ambush

Bakola Ben would sit at Chila Oudhi, camouflaged by the leaves of a drooping branch and tall grass. If an animal passed close enough, on its way to drink, she would pounce on the straggler, usually a chital. But she once nearly caught a careering langur monkey in this way. In an earlier incident in March, watched by astonished tourists, Noon had indeed caught a langur at the lakes. She had charged at a troop of langurs, missed, and retired under a bush. The troop had moved on but one inquisitive monkey had returned to double check. It passed by the bush and she made a successful sideways jack-in-the-box attack.

Surprise Charge

From Chila Oudhi, Bakola Ben could observe the ungulates in the open nala at Chila Pani, about 80-100 metres away. With her keen eyesight, she could pick out the animals quite easily, but being camouflaged herself, they could not make her out. Resting but ever watchful and alert, she would begin stalking. Using any cover she could find, she would work her way opposite the pool from where she was unable to see the animals and they couldn't see her. Nearby, there is an animal trail which leads into the nala, but once in the nala she would be exposed. So peering out from near the trail, her body hidden, she would wait for her chance. At the opportune moment, she would take the animal trail and charge, covering 30 metres in the open, hoping that the advantage of surprise would be enough to carry her to the drinking animals without being noticed prematurely. Deer, especially chital, are quite nimble and she would need to get within metres of her target. Whenever she failed, which was often, she would momentarily look sheepish but then get on with drinking water and immersing herself in it. It was interesting to note that the prey animals would return to drink from that pool the next day, despite a tiger having lain in it.

The Classic Freeze, Stalk and Pounce

This technique was useful when Bakola Ben went on a leisurely walk, usually in the cool of the evening. Between raking tree trunks with her claws and squirting bushes, she would keep a lookout for potential prey and, on spotting an unwary animal, she would immediately freeze. She would then backtrack or creep forward, depending on the cover available. The stalk, punctuated by freezes, would last from anything between a few minutes to an hour. Eventually

1. Bakola Ben stalking in open terrain. Her stalks, punctuated by freezes, would last from anything between a few minutes to nearly an hour. When stalking, a tiger's body is seen to be highly elastic as it almost scrapes the ground and glides past obstacles.

2. Walking from the jamun tree grove and arriving at Chila Oudhi, Bakola Ben momentarily freezes and then gallops at top speed along the nala bank and into the nala itself.

3. From a point overlooking Chila Pani, a pool in the nala, we are greeted with the sight of a sambar stag prostate on its belly at the water's edge with Bakola Ben gripping him by his right hind leg.

4. The sambar is struggling to move forwards but Bakola Ben's grip on the Sambar's leg is firm and, in fact, she manages to pull the large stag backwards.

if she had managed to creep within charging distance, she would explode into a short burst of speed, her acceleration almost unbelievable for an animal of her size.

Once, near Semli, we saw Choti remain frozen for forty minutes. We had sighted her on a walk through a lightly wooded valley where the colour was predominantly dark brown. There was a sambar grazing and Choti had approached it head on. Incidentally, given the choice, tigers do not hunt head on. Choti was only 20 meters away when she became aware of the presence of the sambar still with its head down. She immediately froze, her left forelimb held up in the air. Like all deer, the sambar's eyes do not have great resolving power, (neither do tigers' for that matter) and although Choti was exposed, and the feeding sambar did look up a number of times, Choti's coat colour and stripe had served to camouflage her effectively. Moreover, by staying absolutely still, she did not give herself away. But what would have been an incredible kill did not happen. 40 minutes later, another sambar chanced along, couldn't believe its eyes, and after a few seconds hooted. Choti attempted a half-hearted charge and both sambars ran off easily. No matter, for Choti later killed a chital at dusk.

Opportunism

Three times, from Chila Oudhi, Bakola Ben spotted potential prey, with its back to her, and immediately charged at full speed across a distance of 80-100 metres. The second attempt was successful and is detailed below. (The third was ruined when an on-coming vehicle made her swerve and break her run).

16.30

It is the 6th of April and it is hot, nearly 28 deg C. Bakola Ben, who has been resting in the shade of the jamun trees, gets up and begins a leisurely walk towards Chila Oudhi. She looks very thin and we haven't seen her at a kill for the past six days.

16.45

Reaching Chila Oudhi she surveys the nala below, freezes and then gallops at top speed along the bank and into the nala. A few sambar run up the bank and we hear the distinct and mournful cry of a sambar. We follow to a point overlooking Chila Pani, the pool of water in the nala. The sambar is prostrate on its belly at the water's edge with Bakola Ben holding the deer, apparently by the hindquarters.

The silence is shattered by its piercing cry. It is a large male adult, probably marginally heavier than Bakola Ben, and has a terrified look in its eyes. It is visibly struggling to move forward. It is unable to do so, however, because the tiger has the sambar's right hind leg gripped in its jaws. The tug-of-war continues and Bakola Ben actually succeeds in pulling the large, struggling deer backwards.

16.55

The sambar makes a penultimate attempt to escape. With a huge effort it leaps up and attempts to run, the tiger in close attendance. But Bakola Ben seems to have bitten through his leg muscles. She harries him, and after a few metres, he turns towards the pool. The thick mud slows him down and, as he sinks to his knees at the water's edge, Bakola Ben grabs the hind leg once again and settles down besides him. Why doesn't she finish him off? Perhaps she can sense that the stronger sambar is weakening.

She once again begins to pull the sambar away from the water's edge. Dragging the deer is clearly hard work and after only a few metres she rests, still crouching behind the sambar and still with the hind leg tightly gripped in her jaws.

17.00

The sambar makes a final attempt to escape. Struggling to his feet, this time he runs to the right, but he only lasts a few metres for as he changes direction towards the pool, the wet mud again brings him to a standstill. Remarkably, as he sinks down, she yet again fastens to the hind leg and crouches as before.

17.03

Bakola Ben appears to have sensed that the deer has virtually given up for she releases the grip on the sambar's leg and jumps on its back. He instinctively hunches up and totters for a second as the tiger slides up its back and goes for the neck. As she does so, the sambar topples and they both fall in the thick mud, the sambar almost on top of Bakola Ben. Has she transferred the grip to the throat? It is difficult to tell for their heads are half covered in mud. But she has accomplished her task and the sambar's fight is over.

17.10

Bakola Ben makes her way to the pool, snarling occasionally, but at nothing in particular. She looks ferocious. It is an unfamiliar tiger we are watching now. She sits in the water and continues to snarl. Why?

5. The sambar, with a huge effort, gets up and attempts to run but Bakola Ben harries him, forcing him towards the pool.

6. The thick mud at the pool's edge slows the sambar down and as the stag sinks to his knees the doughty tigress grabs the hind leg once again and settles down behind him.

7. But his bid lasts only a few meters for as he is forced to change direction, the thick mud at the pool's edge yet again brings him to a standstill and Bakola Ben fastens on to his hind leg and crouches as before.

8. Bakola Ben appears to have sensed that the stag has virtually given up the struggle for life for she releases her grip on his leg and jumps on his back.

9. As she applies the killing bite, the hapless sambar topples and falls in the thick, slimy mud.

10. Having killed the sambar, Bakola Ben drags him to the shrunken pool, pausing every now and then, snarling and looking around. The forest is silent.

17.15

Bakola Ben gets up and makes her way slowly to the kill. She stops, looks around, snarls and then bends down to sniff the sambar. Picking him up by the hindquarters, she drags him to the pool. She pauses every couple of meters, snarling and looking around. Is it a warning to anyone intending to steal her kill? The whole area is so silent that it is possible to hear the dragging sound. She enters the pool of water backwards, pulling the sambar into the middle and rests. It is becoming dark and at last she appears relaxed.

But the hard work was not over for her. At around 19.00 she was seen dragging the kill 500 meters - to Jamun Pani from where she had begun her walk at 16.30 - a Herculean task. The next morning, deep in the thicket there was the sound of a tiger eating fragile bones. It was Daku. Bakola Ben was lying in the grass, looking only slightly more full than before. But she seemed unperturbed. There was no sign of the cub.

Tiger's Versatility at Hunting

Did we learn anything new about tiger hunting? One puzzle was that Bakola had water and prey yet Bakola Ben might go without food for several days. Certainly there was less cover than in previous years but there is always good cover in Bakola. So why did she miss meals? One explanation is that if a predator concentrates on an area for too long then the prey animals learn of its presence and become extra alert. Furthermore, a lot of prey animals means a lot of detecting eyes, ears and noses. Additionally, the forest-dwelling animals of Bakola were remarkably co-operative. Because of poor visibility in forests, animals make greater use of sound. A sambar's call warning of the presence of a tiger will be heard all over Bakola. And there was never a shortage of langur, chital and sambar calls in the area.

A new theory is an idea concerning intelligence in hunting. Two levels of intelligence can be distinguished. A predator can learn by making a sequence of connections. The tiger's classic hunting technique is a good example: five-stage operation - freeze, stalk, rush, catch and bite - in which every stage is connected. A young tiger learns these stages by watching its mother hunt and by practice. The other level of intelligence involves taking in a new situation as a whole and then reacting to it appropriately. Tigers are not supposed to charge at full speed over a long distance yet Bakola Ben did that when the situation warranted, and successfully too. Surely it is not too far-fetched to say that tigers can take in and react to unique situations? Since it was an exceptionally hot period following two years of drought, and since she abandoned resting at

Chila Oudhi as the pool dried up, it was a changed situation for which she had devised a new strategy.

Security

Our observations of Bakola Ben's cub were few and limited. Most of the time Bakola Ben was seen alone and, if she was sighted with the cub, it either promptly made for the bush or bolted for the hills. We could not pick out any distinguishing features or even determine its sex with confidence. Bakola Ben also appeared to drag kills over long distances, suggesting that she normally took kills to the cub instead of the other way round. Compared to the cubs of Nalghati Female, Noon and Laxmi, the Bakola cub was nervous and shy. The explanation may have been the traumatic experience a few months earlier, in which a brother or a sister went missing, never to return, and Bakola Ben herself was wounded. A case of insecurity?

Bhaiyu Again

Through this period Bhaiyu, Laxmi's male cub, was making himself at home in Bakola. He often stretched out beside a pool of water, sometimes with Daku in the vicinity. Why was Bhaiyu edging into the centre of Bakola Ben's home range? The most convincing answer concerns water. The period of March-June in 1988 was much drier than average. In previous years, the Semli area had appeared bursting with tigers but this year tiger activity had ceased from April - Semli had no water left by the end of March. No longer did chital daintily pick their way to drink from the stream and there was no reason for Bhaiyu or Choti to lie in ambush. In contrast Bakola, adjoining Semli and connected to it by a nala,had plenty of water. Also Daku, powerful and commanding, was tolerant of his son. The youngster was about 28 months old and still growing. Although he still kept in touch with Laxmi and his two sisters, especially whenever there was a kill to be taken over, he had, technically speaking, separated from them. Still playful and inquisitive, he was nevertheless acquiring the habits of a solitary adult male, padding in desolate nalas on his own, preferring cover to the open, grudgingly tolerating vehicles. Bhaiyu was striding towards independence. The next stage would be a territory of his own. For the present, Daku was tolerant.

So was Bakola Ben, but only just. We did not observe any interaction between them. And at no time did we observe the cub and Bhaiyu together although Bhaiyu must have been aware of the cub. Furthermore, we did not observe Bhaiyu sharing kills with Bakola Ben and Daku. It was all very puzzling. All four tigers were related to each other and it is also possible that Bakola Ben and Laxmi may have been directly related, although there is no way of finding out. Although there is the impression of social behaviour here, it must be remembered that the packing of the tigers together like this was probably forced by the scarcity of water elsewhere. It was involuntary and temporary for we did not find so many tigers together in Bakola ever again. All this suggests that, if forced to, tigers may co-exist together in a small area. It would be their response of 'adapt and survive'. But it is hardly likely that in normal circumstances they find any advantage in living together. But since situations can change and parks may become the last refuge for tigers, it is an intriguing thought. It also raises the carrying capacity of a park in the short and perhaps even in the medium run.

As the days grew even hotter, the pools receded. The distance between Chila Oudhi and Chila Pani lengthened. Bakola Ben changed her routine. She spent less and less time at Chila Oudhi. Then one day, she abandoned Chila Oudhi altogether - the pool had practically dried up. It became more difficult to keep track of her as she adapted to the changing season and shrinking water surfaces. In May it became unbearably hot as temperatures began to nudge 45 degrees C. The last time we saw Bakola Ben in 1988, she was with her cub. Was she showing it the home range? The cub withdrew, but with some dignity now, walking not running. By way of compensation, Bakola Ben put on a special walk as she picked her way fastidiously along the cliff face of Bakola, a unique tigress at home in the unique Bakola habitat.

The New Season

The park closed with the onset of the monsoon season and re-opened in October 1988 with a bizarre regulation. The park management closed off Bakola to everyone except park officials, their guests and a huge open truck. There were occasional reports of sightings of a tigress but it was not until March 1989 that we positively identified Bakola Ben. Of her cub, we heard nothing more.

In 1990 we were able to visit Bakola more frequently and under our own steam. One hot afternoon when the temperature was reaching the 35 degree mark, we spotted a tigress in a lush shady patch, just outside Bakola. Near her was an adult male sambar kill, probably made at dawn and she had fed a little from the deer's rump. The tigress was Bela, Laxmi's daughter, now over four years old and by appearances an efficient predator. She looked relaxed but when another jeep came along and dared to nudge between her and the kill, she snarled and then charged. The jeep quickly went into reverse and Bela aborted her charge. But her explosive action, accompanied by roaring had been truly frightening.

Tigers of Ranthambhore are generally tolerant of jeeps. However, they may charge for three reasons. One is if a jeep comes too close. The tiger will snarl and growl and if the jeep does not respect its distance it will rush at it. Another reason is a jeep too close to cubs. Lastly, a tiger can be quite aggressive when guarding a kill. Noon, normally very placid in the presence of jeeps, would become intolerant of them if they came too close to her kill. Laxmi, on the other hand, would remain quite unruffled.

The New King

Bela became tranquil very quickly and between resting, groomed herself and drank from the stream nearby. But when another jeep arrived, she immediately got up and began dragging the kill towards the thick undergrowth. Traversing the shady, luxuriant area, the kill got trapped between heavy branches lying on the ground. Bela's reaction was to tighten her grip and tug hard, arching her body and using her forelimbs in support. It was slow work and she moved it only five metres. The jeeps stayed back and so apparently satisfied, she settled down to feed. Presently, her ears pricked up and she glanced to her left. In the fading light, we could make out the shape of a large tiger. It kept its distance and it was too dark to see any details of its face. Bela, though, took no further notice of the visitor.

Next morning, it was a cool 31°C at 6.50 a.m. and the two tigers were still there. Bela looked wary but quickly settled into a relaxed posture. The other tiger, a male, got up and walked beside the stream. He stopped to smell a tree trunk, marked the spot with a squirt, and sat down with his face turned away from us. Bela got up to join him, raking a tree with her claws on her way. As the two sat, the male turned his regal head on its massive shoulders and looked at us directly. He was Bhaiyu, son of Daku of Bakola and Laxmi of Lakarda, and brother of Bela. No longer a playful youngster, he had tremendous dignity as he looked disdainfully at us. He had joined the elite rank of adult male tigers and become a stranger.

Bhaiyu had taken over Bakola, but there was, alas, no way of telling how Bhaiyu had dethroned his father. Most tiger studies indicate that maturing male cubs leave the mother's home range to seek territories of their own. Usually, this is some distance away from the father's domain. Occasionally, however, a father will vacate his territory for reasons unconnected with his maturing male cubs. The father may die, then a maturing male may simply stay on. There is a second possibility. Daku may have abandoned the Bakola portion of his territory and incorporated another area elsewhere. Then, during his absence, Bhaiyu could have consolidated his tentative stake in Bakola by the simple act of regular scent marking. The third possibility is that Bhaiyu could have driven Daku away.

Bhaiyu and Bela were seen together several times in Bakola. The two appeared to live together. Of course they were brother and sister, yet they were also four years old and fully sexually mature. Incest in tigers is not normal. The first mating is usually between strangers and the mechanism which facilitates this is dispersal : young males simply leave the area of birth and seek other vacant areas to occupy. For dispersal to work, space should be available, but in Ranthambhore space is simply not there. The park is completely surrounded by steep hills, and, beyond these human settlements. The tigers of Ranthambhore are cut off. The thought of Ranthambore tigers living in isolation, doomed to inbreeding and perhaps extinction, is a chilling one.

The Neglected Habitat

The 1990 sightings of Bhaiyu were our last. Sadly Bakola, the almost ideal tiger habitat, fell into neglect because of human disturbance. Whenever we went there subsequently we found human footprints criss-crossing the tracks. Daytime sightings of tigers were rare. However, although not in abundance, tiger pug-marks remained suggesting that the tigers had chosen not to show themselves during daylight hours.

And what of Bakola Ben, that patient, dutiful and 'boring' tigress calmly going about the task of hunting? She who had given a glimpse of the ferocious power and strength that is latent in all tigers? She who had suggested that tigers can take in a whole picture and react accordingly, perhaps on another level of intelligence? Yes, a police jeep did glimpse a tigress with two cubs drinking at a dam several kilometres away from Bakola. Perhaps it was Bakola Ben. But she hasn't been seen since.

Daku casts a baleful eye at the camera whilst Bakola Ben continues feeding. Tigers sometimes feed together. In such cases the animals are either closely related, such as mother and offspring, or a courting/resident couple.

Noon & Noorjahan

A TERRITORIAL STRUGGLE AT THE LAKES

The park re-opened for tiger-viewing on 1 October 1988, having closed down for the monsoons. The monsoon rains had been exceptional, as if to make up for the previous three years of drought. Indeed, Ranthambhore looked astonishingly green and the air smelt humid. The lakes were coloured blue once again and there were scattered pools of water all over the park.

The visitors came, anticipating a tiger-viewing feast. By now, the park had built up an enviable reputation for tiger-sightings. Sadly, the bubble of expectation was quickly punctured. At the end of October, the park authorities, in their infinite wisdom, introduced regulations, suddenly and unexpectedly, under the pretext of controlling tourist traffic. These reduced the tracks open to tourist vehicles to only three, restricted the most popular Track 2 to a monstrous truck with 30 passengers, limited the number of tourist jeeps to three per track; and shortened the duration of a game drive in the park to a mere 90 minutes. Perhaps the idea was to shepherd most of the visitors in the truck and to keep a watchful eye on the jeeps milling around the lakes. But the reality was different. At all times of day, park managers were seen taking jeep-loads of VIP guests wherever they wished, all over the park at all times of the day, shaded away from the watchful eyes of the tourists. Were the new regulations devised for their priviledge? There were unfortunate side effects: the empty tourist sites became camping grounds for illegal tree cutters and grass gatherers, and the lakes area was fast turning into a dustbowl.

Most tourists were unhappy. There were a few fist-fights, tempers were raised, and a million angry words exchanged. Gradually, however, because the regulations were illogical and unworkable, the tourists 'adapted' them and got on with the business of observing tigers. The big cats, for their part, did not let anyone down.

The Mystery of Kublai

Tiger events of profound significance were taking place. It took us some time to realize that Kublai had gone and that Ashoka had taken over Nalghati Valley and the lakes area from his father; he was seen regularly, prowling the lakes and Nalghati Valley, scent-marking liberally along the way. How had this happened? It is highly unlikely that Ashoka, less than three years old, would have challenged and defeated his father, for Kublai was bigger and more experienced than his son. In any case, the convention with tigers is for young males to seek home ranges of their own elsewhere. It was probably a case of finders-keepers; Kublai had gone missing and Ashoka had taken over. In trying to discover the whereabouts of Kublai, the park management was of no help at all since it wasn't interested and couldn't be bothered.

As Ashoka ranged freely around the lakes, where was the challenge from Noorjahan's brother? After all, he grew up there and, as late as June 1988, had been sighted there with Noon and Noorjahan. Perhaps he had yielded to the urge to move on. In any case, as with Kublai, there wasn't a single sighting of this young male and, again, the park management wasn't interested.

So, Ashoka's reign began in October 1988. He was in robust health, large for his age, and had swapped the youthful inquisitive expression for the characteristic haunted look of an adult tiger.With his characteristic rapid gait, he would cover enormous distances walking purposefully, on and on through his country.

Dawn finds Ashoka purposefully striding along Rajbagh Lake. On this occasion, he was patrolling his territory, liberally scent-marking during a long walk over several kilometers.

Besides Ashoka, Noon and Noorjahan were also frequenting the lakes ecosystem. Ashoka and Noorjahan were first cousins since their mothers, Nalghati Female and Noon respectively, were sisters. Noon had been the resident tigress at the lakes since 1983 and was still in total command. Noorjahan was 29 months old then and had learnt to hunt solo. However, she still kept in touch with her mother and, for the time being, Noon tolerated her daughter.

A Second Litter

Noon had a successful mating in August 1988. Ashoka would have been 32 months old and only just sexually mature. But no one knows if he was the father. No one knew, either, that Noon was pregnant on a fine late afternoon in October when she was spotted moving along Rajbagh lake. With tigers it's like that - a female looks heavy with cubs only during the last week or two of her pregnancy. It is then, especially when she is resting, that one can also see movements in her belly, cubs kicking or wriggling. So as Noon walked along Rajbagh lake towards Padam lake, she looked agile and very mobile. By evening, she had made her way to Jalra forest, which lies between the two lakes, where she sniffed and marked. Satisfied, she momentarily surveyed her forest before moving on.

Noon's second litter was born sometime in November and the realization of what had happened came as a delightful surprise when her two cubs were first seen scampering for cover in the tiny Jalra forest. The surprise led to widespread joy since Noon was the most popular tigress of Ranthambhore, save perhaps for Laxmi. Not many people, however, saw the family in the first few months; Noon saw to that, for she changed dens frequently, keeping the cubs well hidden. But once a tourist, meditating at Rajbagh lake, almost fell out of his jeep when Noon casually passed by him, a helpless cub dangling from her mouth.

Expert at Small Prey

Noorjahan, 31 months old when Noon gave birth, continued to prowl the lakes. She was almost Noon's size, although less powerful, she was quite energetic, though, and it was quite amusing to see her charge or gallop rather, after sambar over a distance of 50-70 metres in the open terrain of the lakes. She failed hopelessly on every such hunt we saw. Each time she looked surprised at having missed, but she was determined to try again. Perhaps she found it fun too. And she learnt.

Noon pauses at late evening to survey Jalra Forest within Ranthambhore National Park. A careful survey includes sniffing the air and listening with cocked ears.

Meanwhile, she survived by becoming an expert on smaller prey. One morning we watched her gallop after a large sambar which escaped easily although badly shaken. Noorjahan stood amidst the dust longingly watching as the sambar crashed through the trees. Still rooted to the spot, a movement in the Jalra forest caught her eye. Intensely interested, she lifted a foreleg to begin tiptoeing into the forest. A chital doe ran out. She was too fast for Noorjahan but the tigress barely noticed her, she was so intent on her stalk. Noorjahan moved about in the forest, criss-crossing it, sniffing, pausing and looking. But the search failed and she duly emerged to sit on the dirt track. She set up a vigil, peering into the forest. After about 15 minutes, she stiffened. Then moving incredibly fast, she pounced. There was a muffled cry and some scuffling in the tall, dense grass. Then came the sound of bones being crunched. It eventually transpired that Noorjahan had caught her initial target, a chital fawn.

Noon dragging a chital stag along a low wall that bisects Rajbagh Lake. Moments earlier, she had attacked eleven grazing chital and following a sixty meters sprint, caught a desultory male.

A Pond Heron, on the hunt, stealthily moves forward, neck craned and bill poised in readiness.

While Noon's cubs confined her to a small area at the lakes, Noorjahan, unshackled, was ranging extensively. She began to scent-mark the farthest corners. Once her scent-marking was well under way, Noorjahan began to regard many remote portions of the park as her own.

Now and then Noorjahan would show up unexpectedly at the lakes themselves, and once she took us by complete surprise by shooting past our jeep, hard on the heels of a petrified Indian hare. The Indian hare is a good bet for a hungry young tiger since it often adopts the escape strategy of sitting motionless even when only partially hidden. Indeed the normally nocturnal mammal is hard to see during daylight hours, the jeep often has to brake hard to avoid running it over. One often thinks that it would be easy to step down and pick it up. However, the hare always breaks into a frenzied sprint at the last minute.

A Gradual Take-over

During December and January, there was little interaction between the adult daughter and her mother. While Noorjahan was appropriating the farthest reaches of her mother's home range, Noon herself, in-between tending to her cubs, was patrolling only a small area around the lakes. The cubs themselves

The Indian Hare is largely nocturnal. Typically, it will lie in a secluded place throughout the day.

remained elusive, Noon chose den sites with dense cover and the cubs did not venture out during daylight hours.

A cool end to January gave way to a cold February, but by the middle of the month the trend to warmer weather was well under way. In early March, Noon's twins were about four months old and she now began taking them on walkabouts. The cubs were still vulnerable, so she avoided the open areas and still preferred darkness. We were thus left with a considerable number of pug-marks to contemplate. By chance, we got one reasonable sighting, which revealed the cubs as brother and sister.

Then Noon made a decisive move. She took the cubs to the South Western corner of her home range, 1/4 km. away from the lakes. Overlooking the new site, which was well covered with dense vegetation, is the hill on which Ranthambhore Fort stands. The area had water, but prey was scarce so that Noon had to make hunting excursions to the lakes, which usually meant picking her way through the nala in which she had given birth to Noorjahan.

Noon may have made the move in order to minimize any interaction between Noorjahan and the cubs. Noorjahan is unlikely to have posed any threat to the cubs but Noon may have wanted to play safe. In a couple of encounters when they had been alone, Noon had made aggressive threat gestures to which

A painted stork fishing in a dark pool on a clear morning. Another typical Indian bird, the stork patiently grids the pool, sifting through water and aquatic vegetation for something to catch in its beak and then swallow.

Noorjahan had responded submissively. Noon was clearly dominant but it was also evident that Noorjahan had no intention of forsaking the lakes.

Tourist pressure at the lakes may have contributed to Noon's decision to move away. Tourism in Ranthambhore had risen since 1986 and management decisions had compounded the tourist pressure on Noon. Instead of spreading the tourists all over the park, the authorities had cordoned off most areas for their own and their guests' exclusive use. So more tourist jeeps than ever were milling around the lakes.

Specialist Lakes Hunter

Noon was a specialist lakes hunter at that time. After all, she had been the resident tigress at the lakes for six years and had naturally got to know the area well. Hunting in the more open areas around the lakes had meant making spectacular sprints on land, and sometimes even in water, hard on the heels of prey. Thus on the 27th March, Noon sat waiting in the tall grass on the shore of Rajbagh lake. Something caught her eye and she promptly slunk through the grass to re-appear at the head of a narrow man-made wall. This is a metre tall, two metres wide,and 70 metres long and runs across the shallow portion of the lake, right up to Rajbagh Palace sited in the middle. From her vantage point she let fly at the 11 chital that were grazing on the wall and, after a 60 metre sprint, caught one, as usual a desultory male. Noon obviously knew that chital, unlike sambar, avoid water and she had deliberately cut off all escape routes save one. It was a simple trap, effectively sprung. She bit through the neck, sat a while to regain her breath, and then dragged the stag all the way back along the wall and into the tall grass. The next morning, she dragged the kill over 1 km. to the cubs. She had however, not forsaken her opportunism. Just the previous day, she had been walking along the shore of Padam lake, it was raining and a large langur monkey had taken refuge under a bush. Its back was turned. Noon spotted the huddled figure, and immediately sprinted 10 metres separating them. A hare sprang away and the langur shrieked, then Noon emerged, carrying the monkey in her mouth. She retraced her route which, of course, led to the den.

Noon, also hunted in her new area. Here, there was sometimes a change in diet as occasionally domestic cattle drifted in. The grazing of cattle was not permitted, of course, but the management was somewhat lax and so one morning, Noon killed a cow. We were alerted to this event when a distressed grazier reported a missing cow and enquired about compensation. Noon had stowed the carcass on a ledge in the rock-face opposite Ranthambhore Fort. The ledge, covered by shrubs and cactus-like plants, was hidden from view. The next day Noon twice descended down the dry slope to drink from the water collected in a hollow. The first time she had one of the cubs with her, although the cub itself had descended by a circuitous route, sticking to shadows and cover. The second time, in the evening's fading light, both cubs came down. The next morning, we saw crows dive in the ledge and fly out with pieces of meat in their beaks - the tiger family had obviously abandoned the remains of the kill. It is interesting that during our vigil, we had heard Noon roaring now and then. This was puzzling for there was no obvious reason for her to roar.

The Inevitable Encounters

Noon stayed in this area opposite Ranthambhore Fort for the rest of the season. Given the terrain, it was difficult to keep track of her but she and her cubs appeared to be doing well. But while Noon was thus occupied, Noorjahan was fast encroaching into the core area of Padam and Rajbagh lakes. She did travel to the third lake, Malik, and beyond but she always returned quickly to spend long stretches of time in the core area of her mother's home range.

By mid-March, the hot weather had settled in. As the heat mopped up all the scattered water, encounters between Noon and Noorjahan became more likely. A compilation for Noon also set in, for a rather touching reason. Noorjahan was still learning to be a good hunter; whereas Noon was clinically precise in her execution, Noorjahan was awkward. In addition, she still sometimes charged recklessly after large prey and missed. As a result, she clearly favoured the Rajbagh Palace area where small prey flourished in the shady forest clearings. Nevertheless, Noorjahan still thought of Noon as a source of food and sometimes, when hungry she would beat a path to Noon's area, roaring and attempting to seek her mother out. Being anchored by her cubs, Noon must have been relatively easy to contact. However, we never found out what transpired between the two in Noon's new area.

It was a different matter when their paths crossed at the lakes. On the evening of the 19th March, Noon emerged from the nala that took her to the shore of Padam lake. As she walked along the vehicle track, so she left a trail of distinctive pug-marks. Walking past the forest rest house, she entered Jalra Forest and then crossed over, via Mori, to the shore of Rajbagh lake. Meanwhile, we had spotted Noorjahan emerging from Rajbagh palace and walking along the wall to the same shore. Noon and Noorjahan, coming from opposite directions, and unaware of each other, were set on an unexpected collision course. When they met on the lake shore, Noon reacted without hesitation by going for Noorjahan. The two tigresses reared up, roaring, paws

AT A RIVULET FLOWING INTO PADAM LAKE, AN INDIAN HARE SITS MOTIONLESS, ITS WAY OF AVOIDING BEING NOTICED BY PREDATORS, WHILE AN EGRET IS ABSORBED IN EXAMINING THE FLOWING WATER FOR SIGNS OF FLOATING EDIBLES.

Although the common Langur Monkey is mostly arboreal, it often descends to forage.

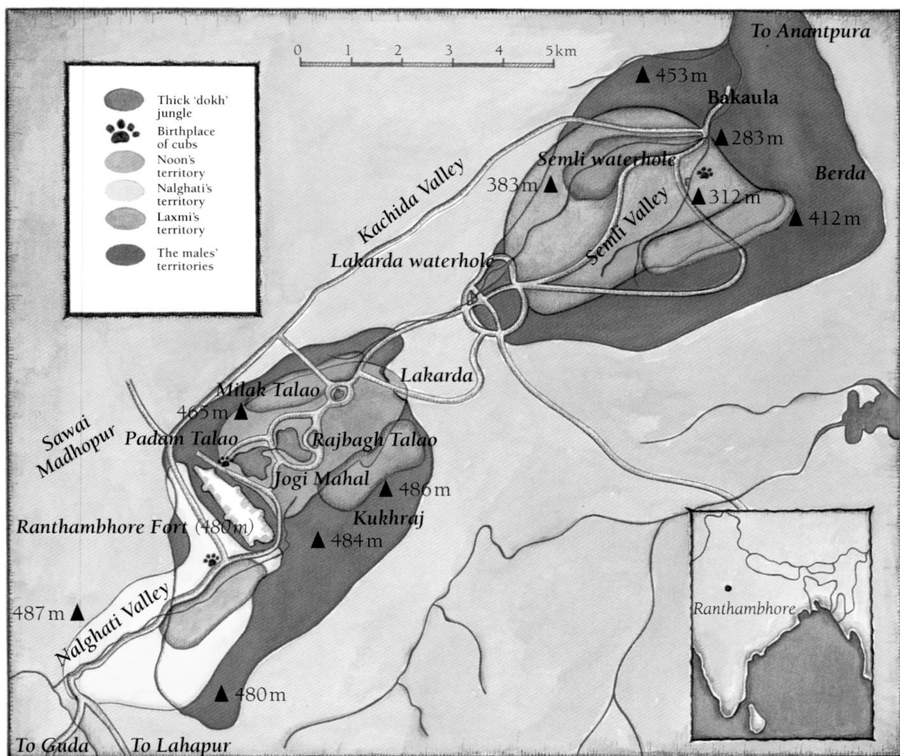

Map to show the female tigers' territories and the range covered by male tigers.

lashing out. The punch-up left Noorjahan sitting submissively in the shallow water as Noon continued imperiously on her way to Rajbagh Palace. After a few long drawn-out minutes, a chastened Noorjahan got up and continued soberly to Padam lake. What could the young tigress be thinking of as she sat on the shore and groomed herself? Again in late afternoon on the 5th April, Noorjahan was sleeping in tall grass, beneath the ruined wall of an ancient building, on the fringe of Padam lake. After a while sambar started calling from a distance and Noon duly emerged from her nala in front of the lake. She padded along the lake shore, seemingly lost in thought. But her reverie was interrupted when Noorjahan shifted in the grass. Noon paused and then lowered her neck, trying to make sense of the movement. Something clicked for she broke into a sprint. The streak of yellow, black and white dived into the tall grass and for half a minute or so, the tigers were not visible. There was much roaring as the patch of grass shook. Then Noon emerged, walking very slowly. After a while, Noorjahan also ventured out, and as the coast was clear, she sat on the lake shore, licking her forelimbs and paws. She looked cool and calm, and seemed unhurt. Perhaps there had been no physical contact, only a noisy family quarrel. Who knows? Cloaked in cover, hidden by the dark of the night, the most telling tiger events even in Ranthambhore, remain shrouded in mystery.

We witnessed one more encounter. On the morning of the 12th April, the noisy crows caught a forest tracker's ears. He eagerly ascended the hill, next to Padam lake, searching for the reason. His descent was pretty quick too, for in the nala he found Noon feeding on a sambar. She stayed with the kill all day, feeding in peace. However, at dusk, the nala reverberated with tremendous roaring. A few minutes later, Noorjahan emerged and walked away quickly. Apparently, she had invited herself to the meal, but Noon had different ideas.

Continuing Separation

The separation of mother and daughter was a drawn out affair and so continued fitfully during April. Perhaps certain types of communication between tigers happen by trial and error, not instantaneously. Noorjahan took time to realize that Noon did not want her around. However, she was determined not to leave the lakes and so dug in. She rested by day in some cool and shady spot, stirring herself into action at dusk. Noon, too, appeared to be settling down in her new area although it was not clear that she would stay on. A sharp reminder of this uncertainty occurred when on the evening of the 20th April we caught a movement in the grass behind the forest rest house at Padam lake. A tail flicked and a muddy face peered through the grass. It was of one of Noon's six month old cubs. The cubs played, using Noon as a giant toy. But the unrelenting April heat made the games too tiring and they curled up between Noon's legs, relishing the security of physical contact. The family was soon fast asleep.

As a sultry April gave way to an oven-baked May, the areas of the two tigresses shrunk further. Noorjahan now hardly left the first two lakes; Noon stepped up her hunting forays to these lakes, where the prey animals were concentrating. But she hardly bothered to scent-mark. In effect, Noorjahan had taken over, at least for this season.

Fading Scents

Noon's 'problem' was that she had to care for her cubs and stay in a limited area, so she could not move around her home range and renew her scent marks regularly. Noorjahan was more mobile and able to probe all parts of the home range. As Noon's scent marks faded, Noorjahan sprayed hers. By this simple act, she was able to stake her claim to the area she had been brought up in, a claim which all tigers, save perhaps Noon, would respect. Note that Noon had not bequeathed her home range; Noorjahan had simply taken advantage of Noon's intermittent presence. So for the time being, the daughter was in charge. However, she would need a year or so in which to consolidate her hold and deal with any late assertion of territorial rights by her mother.

Our map now showed an overlap between the two home ranges; this was a new development for Ranthambhore. Furthermore, Noon was hemmed in on three sides; by Adabalaji Female, Nalghati Beti, and, of course, Noorjahan. Eventually, Noon did extend her home range in the remaining unoccupied area, but for the present there was no point in annexing the vacant land since there was no water there.

The Problem of Packing

One of the problems facing a small, successful national park, surrounded by human habitation, is that its boundaries are set. Early in the park's life this may not matter since the dominant predator population normally starts below the carrying capacity. So the predators tend to have exclusive non-overlapping home - ranges. However, with protection and plenty of prey, the predators increase. In the short run, they may exceed the carrying capacity. They may adjust by 'packing'. i.e. mother and daughter learn to share a home range. Temporarily, the carrying capacity of the park increases.

There is a long term problem, though, if the breeding success continues, since there is a limit to 'packing'. The predators may conflict over territorial rights and may resolve disputes by fights. The outcome is either fatal or the defeated tiger has to leave the park. But here chance encounters between tigers and humans are higher. The park managers then have several options. They can provide incentives for humans to stay away from the buffer area, or incorporate the buffer area into the park. The third option, that of luring the tiger back into the park would, of course, be inefficient. The other options are culling and/or translocation.

While walking through the forest, Noorjahan caught the scent of a spray-mark and immediately proceeded to examine it. She repeatedly sniffed the spot where the spray had struck. Was it some other tiger's or her own? How old was it?

Noorjahan resting in semi-shade near Rajbagh Lake shore. Tigers vary a great deal in their choice of resting place. It depends on circumstances, what's available and the tiger's personality. Some more often choose deep cover whereas others will lie out in minimal cover.

Laxmi's Litter

SECRETIVE LIFE IN MYSTERIOUS LAKARDA

On the first of October 1989, Ranthambore National Park re-opened to tourists, having been closed for the 3 months of July, August and September for the duration of the monsoons. The monsoon rains had been poor and this showed clearly in the state of the lakes; Malik Talao was completely dry and Rajbagh Talao was only half full. The park closes because even with poor rains the roads get muddy and during the latter half of September necessary repair work has to be carried out.

Haunted Tigers

The season started off badly: there was a dramatic fall in tiger-sightings through to December. Moreover, most observations were brief: tiger hurriedly crossing a track, tiger disappearing in a nala, tiger climbing up a steep incline etc. The tigers also appeared more averse to tourist vehicles, moving off at their sound or sight. To all appearances, the Ranthambhore tigers had become circumspect.

One reason was the increase in illegal tree-lopping, grass-cutting and cattle grazing in the park. As the monsoon rains had been poor, and the villages surrounding the park were short of fodder and fuel, a quick solution to the villagers' problems had been to raid the park. From the end of November to 22nd of December, human disturbance was particularly severe. The villagers appeared everywhere, and in Nalghati were accompanied by hired armed dacoits (escorts) to deter the forest department's patrolling guards. There was also a marked absence of rangers on patrol, due to elections. General elections were set for the end of November, to be followed by state elections. In peculiar Indian fashion, forest guards are obliged to report for election duties. So the national parks become vulnerable to raiding parties from the surrounding villages. Another peculiar Indian feature is the atmosphere of lethargy around election time. After elections new faces at the top make new appointments, sack some people and transfer a few others. So government servants 'wait and see', and do little. However, the imminent arrival of a big VIP galvanized the Ranthambhore park management into action and gradually, as the villagers were cleared out, the tigers began to show themselves again.

The Season's New Roll-Call

Which of the familiar tiger faces are around? Noon is seen now and then with her two cubs. Although she has occasionally ventured to the lakes, for the moment she seems settled in her new home range adjoining the lakes. Her adult daughter, Noorjahan, is frequently sighted at the lakes and it looks as if she intends to stay on. She has been busy. Ashoka now about four years old, has been courting her, pug-marks showing that they have walked together over long distances. But probably she has yet to conceive. Ashoka has been doing a lot of straight line walking in Nalghati, Noon's 'new' home range, the lakes, and even Lakarda. His territory now appears to be larger than that of his father, Kublai, whom he has replaced. Is it still expanding? Ashoka's mother, Nalghati Female, has moved right out of the park, to the area around the Rajasthan tourist lodge, and some lucky tourists can sometimes hear her roaring at night. She still has her three cubs with her and the lodge staff once witnessed a male tiger interacting with the foursome. There is water here (the lodge itself draws water from a well) but wild prey is scarce because of thin cover and a lot of cattle grazing and wood gathering. Judging by the footprints, Nalghati Female moves a lot mostly in the dark, catching cattle and the occasional stray camel. Ashoka's sister, Nalghati Beti, is giving fleeting glimpses in Nalghati. So two daughters, Noorjahan and Nalghati Beti, have ousted two mothers with cubs, Noon and Nalghati Female, from their respective home ranges. The Adabalaji Female's cub, Adabalaji Beti is being seen in the Adabalaji area but the mother

Laxmi's female cub, Ladli, gives the mandatory warning snarl before commencing suckling. From the handful we observed, it invariably turned out that male tiger cubs were less shy than female cubs.

A sloth bear caught ambling on a vehicle track in Ranthambhore. Sloth bears are true bears and the name is a historical mistake which has remained; it was originally thought that they were sloths.

has vanished without trace. Adabalaji Beti has not interacted with any human being since the tragic incident of September 1988 in which she killed a boy who had stumbled on her concealed in grass. So that looks like a one-off, which is good news for both humans and tigers.

There is no news of Kublai, nor of Noorjahan's brother. No wonder Ashoka is getting around. Of Bakola Ben, her cub and Daku there have been no sightings at all. There are no reports of Laxmi's three 'Semli' cubs but then the areas of Semli and Bakola remain closed to all non-official traffic. If Daku and Bhaiyu cannot be traced either, that would leave a mystery of four missing adult male tigers. It is a depressing thought.

There is a further puzzle. Strangely, the sightings of sloth bears have gone up dramatically; they are being seen singly or accompanied by one or two cubs. Sloth bears are true bears and the name is a historical mistake which has remained: it was originally thought that they were sloths. An individual weighs between 100-140kg depending on age and sex. These bears feed mainly on insects but they also love ber fruit. There is also an explosion in the sightings of wild boar and peafowl and the peacocks have begun duelling early. Perhaps all this has to do with a decline in the sightings of, not only tigers, but also leopard, striped hyena and golden jackal. But what is the reason? Should there be a connection? Sometimes Ranthambhore can be quite puzzling.

Laxmi's Secret

5th January, 1990. The three cubs peer from under the bushes amidst the tall grass. They look to be nearly four months old. Laxmi is lying flat on the ground on her side, possibly fast asleep. But with Laxmi you can never tell. One cub plucks up courage and advances towards her, slowly and cautiously. Another follows as the first suckles. The third, the female, is more wary. But as she sees her brothers suckling contentedly, she picks her way gingerly through the grass and gives the mandatory warning snarl before muscling in between her brothers. Laxmi sleeps on. There is a faint, warm light on this cool winter day and, apart from the calling of birds, there is silence. At last, Laxmi stirs, yawns and rises. She looks thin. She was obviously looking for prey when she emerged from the steep nala. She moves and the cubs follow. In the grass of the maidan, a flattish area, she sees a chital, stalks and misses. The chital, relieved and excited, calls repeatedly but Laxmi is hardly bothered. She is leisurely making her way to the big Lakarda-Bakola nala, stalking, resting and feeding the cubs on the way.

The Search

That was only our third observation of Laxmi with her three new cubs. But others had seen the family, always in the small Lakarda area. The few brief sightings had been chance events. A tigress with three tiny cubs is very elusive. Normally, during the first two months, the cubs feed solely on their mother's milk and so it is convenient for a tigress to confine them to a den site, in Laxmi's case most probably an inaccessible nala. When the cubs start supplementing their diet with meat, the tigress hunts in the vicinity of the den and tries to take the killed prey back to ithe cubs. Later, she gradually leads them to a kill away from the den and takes them on occasional walks.

Finding Laxmi and her family wasn't going to be easy. In fact, we searched for 20 days and did not see a single tiger. There was a lot of illegal grass cutting, tree lopping and cattle grazing going on in the park, making the tigers lie low. But Laxmi had left clues throughout Lakarda: a flattened patch on the grass with blood clots where she had fed; pug-marks of a tigress accompanied by three young cubs; pug-marks leading into an inaccessible nala from where one

Two peacocks leap high into the air, kicking at each other as they battle for the attention of a nearby peahen. From late March onwards, peacocks dance and court the peahens. They also fight for domination.

Two competing peacocks will face each other, perhaps also circle a little, and then leap up, kicking out with wings stretched. They do this several times before the vanquished gives up and leaves.

could hear her roaring; langur monkeys perched on tall trees, with a view into the nala, giving alarm calls; drag marks along a dirt track ending abruptly at the nala's stony bed; fresh claw marks on tree trunks, and so on. It was frustrating. Yet it was also reassuring to know that the family was around. The weather was pleasant, so it was fun as well.

Then, after three weeks of searching, on the last day of 1989, we saw Laxmi with her three cubs. It was in the evening. The light was soft. There was not a vehicle in sight and there she was, in the lightly wooded maidan or plain ambling along the track to the Kala Pathar nala, with the three cubs in tow. As they approached our stationary vehicle, the cubs became aware of our presence and climbed up the hill on the edge of the maidan, to make a detour to the nala. This reinforced our belief that encounters between them and vehicles had been rare. As they walked hurriedly, keeping their heads low and a watchful eye on our vehicle, they appeared quite small and vulnerable. But Laxmi was as cool as ever. She walked straight on past us, hardly batting an eyelid. As she approached the entrance to the nala, another vehicle arrived on the scene and she disappeared, the cubs broke into a run, and we were left with only a memory to treasure.

Laxmi was about 14 years old then, a minor achievement in survival for a wild tiger. This was her third known litter, to which she had given birth sometime in late September or early October, 1989, most likely in the Kala Pathar nala. Her Semli cubs were born in January 1986, giving an interval of three years eight months, about one year more than the average. Unlike her previous litter of Bhaiyu, Bela and Choti, this litter consisted of one female and two males. Of course, there was no way of telling if Laxmi had given birth to more than three cubs, although zoo studies indicate that the average litter size at birth is between three and four cubs. Zoo observations can also, of course, identify the father. Now judging by the pug-marks, there was only one male tiger frequenting the Lakarda area and the prints matched those of the ubiquitous Ashoka. Unfortunately, we never saw him with the family, which spent most of its time in inaccessible nalas. But we often found his pug-marks going in and out of the same nalas. It seemed certain that he had annexed Lakada and incorporated it in his territory.

Lakarda

Keeping track of Laxmi was tricky. Lakarda is the site of the former village of the same name. Today, its ruins stand on the slope of a low hill. When Ranthambhore was incorporated into India's Project Tiger in 1974, the first task had been to re-settle its villagers. The Lakarda area, the core area of Laxmi's home range, is essentially three big nalas (dry river beds) separated by maidans (stretches of flattish areas) and low hills. Bordering Lakarda is the three kilometre long Malik Talao Anicut-Lakarda nala, and as the name implies, it runs from the Malik Talao to Lakarda. There is the interruption of an open area between this nala and its continuation, the nine kilometre long Lakarda-Bakola nala. At the opposite edge of Lakarda is the third nala, the Kala-Pathar nala. Whereas the other two nalas are wide with occasional steep sides, the Kala-Pathar nala is uniformly narrow and runs steeply up into the hillside. It is dominated by huge slabs of black stones, hence the name Kala Pathar (black stone). The maidans and the low lying hills sandwiched between the nalas contain tall grass and plenty of bushes, dense in places. The maidan which spreads out in front of the Kala Pathar nala is wooded and is dimly lit. There are also a couple of water holes in the maidans but they tend to dry up quickly. However, there are two wells from which water is drawn to fill the water-holes from April to June. But this year the wells dried up as well and digging began in April to get at the water further down.

Nala Movements

The family spent most of its time in the nalas and regularly changed nalas. A discernible pattern gradually appeared and it turned out to be a simple one. At first the family would be residing in, say, the Kala Pathar nala. Confirmation would be provided by the sounds - the tiger roaring and sambar and chital giving out alarm calls. Furthermore, from the higher hill opposite, through binoculars we could occasionally glimpse the tigers drinking from one of the three visible hollows in the nala. If Laxmi had managed to kill in the nala, the family would stay for a few days, feeding, drinking and lazing. Laxmi would occasionally move out of the nala in the dark and return before dawn. Once the family had demolished the kill, Laxmi would venture out alone, to hunt. If successful, she would drag the kill to the nearest nala. The kill would be stored in a cave or a rock shelf, and would be quite safe, as there appeared to be hardly any jackals or hyenas around, and vultures were unlikely to sight the stored kill. The only animal likely to appropriate the kill was Ashoka. Laxmi would then return to Kala-Pathar Nala to lead the cubs across the maidan junction to the kill. However, if Laxmi's hunt was unsuccessful, she would still return, leisurely, to Kala Pathar nala to collect the cubs to accompany her on her second hunting foray. Why the change-over? It turned out that the prey animals got to know the family's presence in a particular nala if they stayed there for too long. It was on such second hunting sorties that we would usually catch the family together.

Of course, there were variations on this central pattern. Sometimes Laxmi would kill more than once in or near one nala and so stay there longer. Sometimes the unexpected would happen. Once looking through binoculars and expecting to find Laxmi and her cubs, we picked up a man taking a bath, complete with soap, at one of the three visible Kala Pathar hollows. Then he calmly proceeded to wash his clothes, sit down and smoked a cigarette. Finally, he gathered up his belongings and moved on. We surmised that he was a dacoit on the run. Laxmi, taking no chances, had left the nala in a hurry.

Why did Laxmi make such heavy use of the nalas? Now, the herbivores of Lakarda forage in the maidans, woods and hill slopes but, given the scarcity of water, have to take recourse to entering the nalas to drink where permanent water is found. This gave Laxmi the opportunity to ambush prey animals. The nalas also provided places where Laxmi and her cubs could eat in shade. With water, food, shade and Laxmi's skills, they provided an almost self-contained habitat, if not for a long period, at least for many days.

Stalking or Charging

Laxmi came out primarily to kill prey. It looked as if she could not kill in the nalas on a sustainable basis and so some supplementation was required. Outside the nalas, there is plenty of cover afforded by bushes, shrubs and tall grass and, in places, the vegetation is quite dense. This is probably why Laxmi is a stalker. It is difficult to imagine her charging over long distances in the

Kati Nak, Laxmi's bold male cub, poses on a fallen tree trunk after having investigated it thoroughly. At this age, 6-7 months, the cubs are highly curious about their environment.

Rajbagh Lake's water surface is in turmoil due to wriggling, rolling and twisting muggers or marsh crocodiles. Since the crocodiles' teeth are not sharp enough to tear the hide of a freshly killed sambar, they attempt to break off chunks, to be swallowed whole.

Greylag geese taking off. These winter visitors to Ranthambhore spend most of the day resting around the lakes, but in the evening they take off in large flocks to feed in farms surrounding the park.

Lakarda landscape. Bakola Ben sometimes resorted to charging as did Noon, hunting in the relatively open terrain around the lakes. In contrast, Laxmi crept as close to the intended victim as possible.

Threats to Tigers

There were other possible reasons for Laxmi's preference for the nalas. One concerns the threat from other animals. In all tiger history only one instance has been recorded where crocodiles killed an inexperienced tiger that had entered water. In Ranthambhore, there are many muggers (marsh crocodiles) inhabiting the lakes but no case of a mugger killing a tiger has ever been recorded. In fact, in every tiger-crocodile encounter in Ranthambhore, the crocodile has come off worse. One evening in early 1988, Noon and her two cubs had been spotted at the lakes. That night people in the forest rest house heard tiger roars and growls. Next day, there was a dead crocodile with tiger hair stuck to the bloody wounds on its underside. Three sets of tiger pug-marks were also evident. On land, tigers must have crocodiles at a disadvantage, but when entering water in Ranthambhore's lakes, tigers, especially cubs, will give warning snarls to the water surface and proceed cautiously. Most tigers also avoid sloth bears if they can, although sloth bears are short-sighted and often blunder into tigers. Once in early 1989, Noorjahan was sitting on the track when a sloth bear ambled around the corner. It stopped at 15 metres upon seeing the crouched tigress, and stood up on its two hind legs in a threat gesture, whereupon Noorjahan crept away. But Gengis, the adult male tiger at the lakes in 1983 and 1984, was intolerant of sloth bears and once attacked and chased a bear that had walked past the bush under which he was resting.

With tiger cubs it is a different matter. When left unguarded, they run a variety of risks. Very young cubs can be picked up by large birds of prey. Slightly older cubs can be devoured by jackals. Cubs that are a month or two old are vulnerable to leopards and striped hyena. So a tigress tries to leave her un-guarded cubs in a safe place. The nalas were Laxmi's solution to the problem of security. There were many caves, crevices and sheltered places in the nala walls where she could leave her cubs in relative safety. Her regular changing of nalas also prevented the build up of smell and other evidence of the cubs' presence.

Finally, there was a particular reason for Laxmi to stick to the nalas- human disturbance. The grass gatherers who came to Lakarda worked in parties of 8-12, men and women. They sang to keep their spirits up and frighten off any predators. The villagers timed their entry and exit well, they entered before the tourists got going and left during the afternoon rest period for the park. If accidentally encountered by tourists, some grass gatherers would run off, some would nonchalantly continue cutting grass and some would even throw stones.

Fortunately for tigers, nalas contain little vegetation so that they were of little use to human beings. Their value, as discovered by Laxmi and the bathing dacoit, was as a hiding place from human disturbance. Laxmi's use of nalas in Lakarda had been multi-purpose and for us it had been a revelation.

Getting to Know the Tigers

Sometimes Laxmi and her family changed nalas quickly, at other times leisurely. It was in the latter cases that we really got to know the family.

Early one April morning around 7.15 a.m. Laxmi and her cubs emerged from the Kala Pathar nala and stepped into the wood. Although it was very warm, 28°C, the cubs had eaten and they were in an exploratory mood. The bold male cub with a cut across his nose, called Kati Nak (cut nose), led followed by his sister, called Ladli (mother's favourite), alongside Laxmi, with the other male cub, Radar, bringing up the rear. As usual, Laxmi decided to take it easy and promptly sat down. Kati Nak took the greatest of interest in a fallen tree trunk, and having exhausted all possibilities, flopped down beside it, panting with his tongue well-out. He was joined by Ladli and the twosome stood hesitant, snarling together side by side, before venturing to join Laxmi.

Laxmi was interested in hunting but that did not distract her from spraying a few prominent tree trunks and once getting up on her hind legs to rake a tree with her claws - fresh signs of occupancy of her home range were going up. As Laxmi moved, the cubs kept up with her, stopping when she stopped, walking with her and under her as she walked, starting in the direction in which she stared, but all with a detectable time lag so engrossed were they in everything around them. Gambolling alongside their dignified mother, they would get distracted by the real and the imaginary, play catch, block Laxmi, bump into her if she stopped, rub their heads under her chin, and 'help' her hunt. When

A Crested Serpent Eagle waits on a tree branch, having just caught a snake. The crest of this eagle can be erected like a ruff.

Laxmi dragging a wild boar carcass. When we chanced upon a reclining Laxmi with this kill, she had already eaten a little of the rump. Inexplicably, the tiger family left most of the wild boar uneaten.

Laxmi saw a chital 100 metres away, she hunched with a forepaw held up and froze. Kati Nak caught up with Laxmi, nuzzled her and also picked out the chital. Without hesitation he took off after the chital joined by Ladli. The chase ended in failure with a badly shaken chital warning every animal in the vicinity of the tigers' presence. Laxmi took the opportunity to retire under the shade of a tree.

Now about seven months old, the cubs had a lot to learn. They were growing fast and very energetic, highly mobile and roaming greater distances. On walkabouts with their mother, they explored with little restraint and investigated virtually everything that caught their attention. But not only were they very curious, they were also highly alert, watching and observing prey and the way their mother hunted. It is by visual observation first and practice later, that tiger cubs acquire the skills of hunting. Unfortunately, in this first phase of learning to hunt, they are a nuisance to the mother, often getting in her way and spooking the prey.

Laxmi's cubs were certainly unable to contain their exuberance at being alive and fit on such a fine morning for they were off again, chasing a langur

Kati Nak and Ladli stand together side by side, hesitant and snarling, before venturing to join their reclining mother, Laxmi. If separated from their mother, the cubs became somewhat nervous of vehicles.

monkey which promptly climbed up a tree, followed by the determined but futile efforts of Radar and Ladli to climb the tree as well. But as the temperature edged past 30°C at 9 a.m., the cubs decided to rest alongside Laxmi under the shade of trees. Even as they flopped down, it was with an air of forced rest. Sitting and panting, they radiated an air of readiness, eager for action.

During such walkabouts, Laxmi was never observed to display annoyance or anger. Neither cub got reprimanded in spite of hindering her efforts to hunt. She made no conscious effort to discipline them to lie low or stay put while she stalked. There must have been pressure on her to hunt something sizeable every two or three days, yet she took all the boisterous activity in her stride. It was noticeable that the cubs followed her actions and tried to mimic her hunt. Perhaps when she hunted with the cubs in tow, it was more a demonstration for their benefit - a lesson. She preferred to do her serious hunting alone.

During another nala change-over, which took place just before dawn, Laxmi killed a wild boar and dragged it to a secluded place. The Indian wild boar is killed and eaten regularly by Ranthambhore tigers. The wild boar has weak eyesight, average hearing and lacks speed, but it has an acute sense of smell, formidable tusks, very strong teeth and good agility. It is also courageous. Given a choice between an adult boar or a youngster, tigers often go for the latter, an indication that adults are not to be taken lightly.

At 7.30 a.m. we found Laxmi sitting a little distance away from the kill. The cubs were nearby on top of a bush-covered hillock. The wild boar carcass was intact; it looked healthy and did not smell. Yet Laxmi was in no hurry to feed. It gradually transpired that there was something strange about the carcass as far as the tigers were concerned. After a while, Laxmi walked to the kill. She did not look full. She picked up the carcass in her jaws, dragged if for about 10 metres, and then shook it. Dropping it to the ground, she began to pluck hair out of the boar, but after ten minutes gave up and sat down. When she eventually started feeding from the hindquarters, it was more like nibbling. Having eaten a little, she moved about 15 metres away to rest and sleep. Clearly, there was something unappealing about the wild boar but there were no clues for us to work out what it was.

Radar descended first and after greeting Laxmi, approached the kill. He, too, did not look full but left the kill after eating a few mouthfuls. It was too hot for Radar to explore so he flopped down with an audible grunt besides his mother. Although fully prone, Laxmi was keeping an eye on the kill. The half-closed eyes opened up in a flash when a tree pie landed on the carcass. Laxmi was up and charging, eyes flashing and fixed intently on the tree pie. The bird flew away but Laxmi snarled, growled and displayed real anger before she returned to her place of rest. Such anger was very rare in this tigress. It was a vivid reminder of the ferocity which tigers possess but rarely reveal.

In spite of her protective attitude to the kill, none of the four tigers made any impression on it. The cubs approached it individually, but did not stay for long. Laxmi did not even bother. Then, in the cool of the evening, Kati Nak initiated the departure. We never learnt why they had rejected the wild boar.

The last time we saw the family together was on a peaceful evening in the summer when the midday wind is as hot as an oven's blast and evenings are ideal for sunbathing: 30°C at 6.00 p.m. Four bulging shapes managed to come out of the Lakarda - Bakola nala. Predictably, Kati Nak was way out in front, followed by the imperial Laxmi accompanied by Ladli, and a meandering Radar brought up the rear. In Laxmi's family, Ladli was the smallest and perhaps therefore lacked confidence. Staying close to Laxmi probably gave her additional security. But Kati Nak appeared to have a mind of his own and was insatiably curious.

Laxmi, half-sleeping, momentarily opens her eyes. Resting near her kill, the tigress is always on alert for anything that may chance to interfere with the carcass.

Laxmi flopped down at the mouth of the nala and Ladli tucked in beside her. Radar continued exploring, using all the three senses of smell, sound and sight. He was eventually rewarded when he came across a square piece of flat rubber which he picked up in his mouth, sat down, and got engrossed in giving it a thorough examination. He chewed it, teased it, pawed it and generally thought that there was considerable life lurking within it. The piece of rubber had once been a flap at the rear of a tourist jeep. Watching Radar was interesting, but it was also rather shocking, this intrusion of a man-made item in a wild tiger's mouth. Meanwhile, finding our vehicle interesting, Kati Nak walked up to it directly, his head bobbing up and down, peering to see the interior. When it seemed as if he was about to climb in, Radar spotted and chased a peacock and Kati Nak joined in the lost cause. It is likely that their eventual first kills would be peacocks, followed by hares and then fawns. Returning, Kati Nak got distracted by the piece of rubber and tried to finish Radar's task of bringing it to life.

Rear view of a displaying peacock. Peacocks are closely associated with India and are found all over Ranthambhore. Their presence and behaviour adds an exotic touch to the forest.

The relationship between the family and vehicles was an interesting one. Laxmi, now about 15 years old, had been used to the presence of vehicles since the age of six months. Although she was difficult to sight, frequenting areas where jeeps could not go, when she was 'caught' by tourist vehicles, she appeared not to take any notice. She reminded us of an accomplished diplomat who puts on the best behaviour in public, never once giving the hint of wishing to get away from onlookers. But the cubs were shy of vehicles, and we made four interesting observations concerning their behaviour. First, at the sound of approaching vehicles they would immediately bolt for cover. In time, however, they would very cautiously return. Second, the first to come out of hiding was always Kati Nak, usually followed by Radar. Third, they never came out of hiding if Laxmi was absent. Finally, the number of vehicles made a difference (and probably the behaviour of the occupants made a difference as well). When ours was the only vehicle around, seemingly lifeless, the cubs would be very active, although they always kept a wary eye on us. Sometimes curiosity would get the better of fear and Kati Nak or Radar would approach the vehicle to inspect it, heads raised and eyes peering.

An interesting observation on this last evening was that Laxmi was the centre around which the cubs were active and that they made it a point to register physical contact with her now and then. It was as if a puppeteer was holding invisible strings, drawing a puppet in whenever it strayed too far. We reluctantly left the family in fading light in front of the grand Lakarda - Bakola nala. It would have been indecent to linger on: We were a total irrelevance in this natural setting. The next morning, there were four sets of footprints leading into the Kala-Pathar nala and, so, that was that; the monsoons came and the park closed again.

Other Ranthambhore Events

The 1989 - 1990 viewing season had seen some unusual non-tiger events. One morning, a stray dog appeared at the park gate, and as it approached, the guard lashed out with his leg. The rabid dog bit him on the leg and the chest, and escaped into the park. The dog made it to the lakes, its progress traced by langur and chital calls. The animals stared hard and tentatively followed this strange creature they had probably never seen before. The dog had a free run of the park and spent its time chasing chital and barking at langurs, before leaving of its own accord. The next morning, it savaged a jeep driver who, with the help of another, had bare-handedly attempted to tie a scarf round its muzzle. The dog wandered into the park again and we spotted it at the lakes, sitting near a few peacocks and looking longingly at a few langurs upon a tree. It tried to bite the tyres of tourist vehicles and wandered off, chasing amazed chitals. It was not until the next evening that the park management got round to shooting it in Nalghati Valley.

Another morning, a jeep driver saw drag marks on a dusty track. He got down from the jeep and followed the drag marks which led into grass. Tracing drops of blood and the places where the grass had been flattened, he came to a chital kill, barely eaten. By chance, he looked up and saw Noon staring at him from a height, 25 metres away. He hurriedly scrambled back to the jeep. An hour or so later, two young forest employees came on foot. Their duty was to draw water from a nearby well and fill up a water-trough. They, too, investigated the kill. Then came the jeeps with the tourists in the afternoon. It was not until 4 p.m., when all but one jeep had left, that Noon came out of hiding and dragged the kill away.

A tree-pie has landed on Laxmi's wild boar carcass and, in a flash, Laxmi is up and charging, eyes intently fixed on the little carnivorous bird.

One noteworthy tiger event sticks in the mind. One cool and misty morning, we checked that the pug-marks of Laxmi's family were leading into the Kala Pathar nala. Just to be sure, we drove slowly around the Lakarda area, looking for the distinctive tiger tracks. Passing by the waterhole before the entrance to the Lakarda - Bakola nala, a peacock hurriedly took off from a tree just inside the nala walls. We stopped and a few minutes later a tiger emerged. It was a little disconcerting to see the tiger for we had been confident that Laxmi was in the Kala Pathar nala. But it wasn't Laxmi, it was Choti, Laxmi's daughter from her Semli litter of January 1986, now about four years old. She was walking towards Kala Pathar nala but stopped three times to scan for prey. As she walked through the wood before the nala entrance, she roared. And then there was an answering roar from the right, whereupon, Choti immediately veered to the left and climbed up away from Kala Pathar nala still roaring. There were a few more responding roars from Laxmi, until, Choti could be heard no more. It was indeed Laxmi at the nala entrance, with the three irrepressible cubs playing around her, who had been replying to Choti. Laxmi then went back into the nala. The family stayed in the nala throughout the day. Two days later, we saw Choti again in Lakarda. There seemed little doubt that Choti and Laxmi recognised each other yet had mutually avoided closer contact. Still, Choti and Laxmi had demonstrated respect for each other's privacy with a marvellous touch.

The last time Laxmi's cubs were seen together was in September 1990 when the cubs were about a year old. Following the monsoon rains, they had moved to the hills. There was a commotion and a cub was seen being chased by a sloth bear. But the tables were turned when the other two cubs arrived and the three of them teamed up to chase the bear out of sight. After that, during the October 1990 - June 1991 season, the cubs were seen singly or in a pair, always in or near the Lakarda area. But that season sightings of Laxmi had ceased by November. It was mysterious.

An important tiger event had also occurred in early March 1990; Noorjahan had given birth to three cubs.

Right, a new born Common Langur infant, already adept with its hands. Langurs are the only primates living in Ranthambhore.

Left, Laxmi affectionately licks her male cub Radar. Whenever unsure, a cub will seek out its mother for reassurance.

Noorjahan's Family

GLIMPSES INTO LITTLE KNOWN ASPECTS OF TIGER LIFE

Looking down from a height of 25 metres, the tiger was in clear view: forelimbs spread out and head lowered to drink, using his tongue to lap the water backwards into his mouth. Interesting to note that the tiger's head was clear of the water, unlike a dog who submerges its muzzle in water and drinks by lapping forwards. It was Ashoka drinking from the pool of water in the Malik-Larkada nala, 15 metres away from the man-made wall that dammed the water on the other side. This is exactly on the border that separates Laxmi's Lakarda home range from Noorjahan's Lakes home range. It is also at this point that Noon's home range overlaps those of the other two. Ashoka's presence here was emphatic; he was the only male tiger to be seen in these three home ranges. Nalghati Beti's home range also fell within his territory. Laxmi and Noon were older than him, Noorjahan was younger, and Nalghati Beti was his twin. Clearly, this four year old male's empire building had gone extremely well, in such a short space of time. But where were the other male tigers?

He did not seem to mind that there were over 60 people watching him from more than 10 vehicles parked haphazardly on the wall of the dam. Indeed he proceeded to sit in the water, entering backwards in the usual tiger fashion. He looked completely full but where was the kill? He sat unperturbed for a long time, occasionally lapping water. Then, getting up leisurely, he walked towards Malik Talao, scent-marking on the way. Past the Talao, he scrambled up the crumbling wall of an ancient ruin, almost slipped, and then walked into the Kukraj nala in Noorjahan's home range. Possibly the kill was somewhere in the nala. Two days later, he appeared again at the same place and repeated the drinking and sitting performance. But this time he left via the Malik-Lakarda nala, scent-marking bushes and also luxuriating in pools of water on the way. Perhaps Laxmi might have a carcass he could poach.

Noorjahan's Secretive Behaviour

It was Ashoka who was responsible for Noorjahan's three cubs. During March 1990, Noorjahan's behaviour had changed in pattern. The previous month she had been seen often. Apart from Ashoka, she was the only other tiger to be seen at the lakes where tourist vehicles congregate. She had been observed frequently, relaxed and tolerating semi-circles of vehicles. In early March, she became furtive and rarely sighted by day. People started speculating, since she was the tourist attraction. Was she simply avoiding the heavy tourist traffic? But then it was noticed that she was utilizing only a tiny portion of her home range, confining her movements to a place called Jalra very near the Park Gate between Padam Talao and the entrance to the Nalghati Valley. Was she restricting her movement because of the scarcity of water and prey? But upon reflection, this was thought implausible since there were a number of places in her home range with water, prey and cover.

Noorjahan fooled everyone because nobody got a good look at her in the first half of March. Had she allowed a proper viewing, it would have been noticed that she had a bulging belly - pregnant tigresses only show the swollen belly during the final week or two of a pregnancy that lasts for 105 days on average. During the last few days an expectant tigress is occupied in looking for and checking out suitable den sites. She also rests a lot since it cannot be easy to sustain energy levels in that condition.

Noorjahan gave birth in Jalra. In places the vegetation is impenetrable, providing excellent cover and protection. There is also water nearby and prey within easy reach. The cubs were born between the 9th and the 15th of March 1990.

Ashoka quenching his thirst at Malik Dam. When they are feeding, tigers usually drink large quantities of water. Often a tiger will drag the carcass of a large victim a considerable distance to water before beginning to feed.

The Birth of Baby Tigers

A tigress normally takes about an hour to deliver. She may have more than three cubs. But there are stillbirths, and cub mortality is also high in the first few days. So we do not know how many cubs a wild tigress actually delivers. After delivery, the tigress eats the after-birth. On average, the ratio of male to female is even. Tiger cubs weigh between one and two kilogrammes at birth but they put on weight fast. They are born blind and open their eyes after about two weeks. During this initial period of complete helplessness the mother helps the cubs find her teats, prevents them from wandering away and keeps them together as much as possible. There is a lot of physical contact involved and cubs use their sense of smell to locate their mother as well as each other. The tigress also keeps the cubs warm, getting them to huddle next to her body. She licks and grooms them regularly which stimulates blood circulation and promotes urination and defecation. Repeated physical contact also enables a bond to develop between mother and cubs. Although the cubs have a full set of milk teeth when they are about four weeks old, they feed solely on the mother's milk for nearly eight weeks. After that, they start adding solid food to their diet. By then, they also begin to see clearly. In the early days the tigress spends most of her time at the den with the cubs, leaving only for short periods to drink or hunt. So her home range shrinks dramatically.

When we first saw Noorjahan on 20th March, she was alone, looking for prey and her teats were full of milk. Not until the 10th April was she seen with the cubs, later identified as two males and one female. She was resting and small shapes were glimpsed sliding over her belly. For the next week or so, she was again seen alone looking for prey. Then on the 18th of April she was spotted, carrying her cubs, one by one, in her mouth. They were then about five to six weeks old and she was changing den sites.

During the first eight weeks or so, a tigress changes den sites several times. The idea is to prevent a build up of tiger smell and other evidence of the cubs' presence. There are a few predators - leopard, striped hyena, golden jackal - who can make a meal of tiger cubs, but probably the biggest danger is from a roving male tiger. The tigress also changes den sites if she feels disturbed.

Her face contorted with fury, Noorjahan snarls and growls at a tourist climbing on top of his vehicle to obtain a better view. The cubs are unaware of the distraction and continue playing around their mother.

Noorjahan flicks her tail close to a cub, inviting the youngster to trap it, and then neatly flicks it away. The cubs found this game utterly fascinating. They also loved it when Noorjahan swishes her tail over them, enticing them to leap up to catch it.

An Evening Performance

On 24th April Noorjahan deposited the cubs in the Kamaldhar caves. The miniature Kamaldhar Gorge begins at a sharp corner on the track that unwinds itself in Nalghati Valley. At the corner of the track, looking immediately below on the left, is the gorge with steep sides. In the wall of the opposite side are a few caves, call them cub caves, at floor level. On the floor itself there is a pool of water, with vegetation and a few scattered boulders. To the right of the cub caves and near the top, there is a gentle slope covered with grass and trees. The gorge itself narrows considerably a little further on down into a nala which drops precipitously and continues for a few kilometres, with the vehicle track always on the right of it. About 100 or so metres from the caves and in the far side of the nala are a few caves, call them tiger caves, where Noorjahan herself often curled up and went to sleep.

On the morning of the 26th, Noorjahan was sleeping in one of the tiger caves and the cubs were inside one of the cub caves. At midday, lured by a jeep driver's mimicking of tiger roaring, the cubs came out one by one but then quickly retreated back to the cave. At 4.45 p.m. all three cubs were wide awake, two sitting just outside the cave, waiting in anticipation. Half an hour later, peacocks started calling from the nala. And then it came - *aaaoou, aaaoou* - the haunting sound of a tiger roaring, reverberating against the Valley walls. The vocalization was continuous, each roar punctuated by only a few seconds of silence. At about 5.30 p.m. Noorjahan appeared and paused to take in the scene. Satisfied, she climbed up the gorge wall to the open grass patch. There she sat down, all four legs spread out on one side, commanding and authoritative.

The cubs were excited but directionless. But with one more prompting call from Noorjahan, they were able to locate her. Running and scrambling, the male cub in the lead bounded up and then flung himself at her. There was a lot of mutual nuzzling and licking. He had clearly missed her. The other two cubs caught up and there was more joyous greeting. As Noorjahan sat, licking and comforting the cubs, they appeared to go mad. They hurled themselves at her body, her head in particular, climbed all over her and zestfully examined every feature of her anatomy. Can a mother mean so much? The cubs were especially fascinated by Noorjahan's tail and she knew it. She would flick her tail close to a cub, inviting it to catch it. But as soon as the cub made contact, she would flick it away. Sometimes she would flick the tail right over the cubs, causing them to leap up to grab it.

The distance separating the tiger family and the few vehicles on the track was only 200 metres, although of course the big gap of the gorge lay in between. Noorjahan had probably learnt by experience that vehicles cannot cross such gaps and so was quite relaxed, but she did check on the vehicles continually. Then the spell was shattered when a jeep occupant further back stood up to get a better view. Noorjahan's benign, almost soppy expression changed to one of contorted fury as she got up snarling and growling. Unaware of the disturbance, the cubs dutifully followed their mother who climbed up a further 20 metres to a patch of grass amidst trees and bushes. She settled down quickly and in due course the cubs suckled. They then went exploring in the vicinity of their mother. They attempted crazy activities, like climbing a small bush, but regularly returned to make physical contact with Noorjahan. It was reminiscent of the behaviour of Laxmi's cubs on the last day we saw them together at the mouth of the Lakarda-Bakola nala. But there was a difference. Noorjahan's cubs' physical contact included climbing all over her and boisterously playing all around her. Throughout, Noorjahan stayed in the same spot, grooming herself and the cubs. Thus occupied, we left the family at seven in the evening.

What we had witnessed was something special. There were at least three factors which had combined to produce the scene: habituation, heat and space. Over an exposure of three years, Noorjahan had come to accept the presence of vehicles and had worked out that vehicles were harmless. Then there was the exceptionally hot April and May. The temperature in early May lingered at 35°C even at 5.30 p.m. The days were usually cloudless and the midday heat was unbearable. It was probably cooler in the shaded cub caves at floor level in the gorge. Many pools and water-holes had dried up and prey was congregating near whatever water was available. Noorjahan needed to be near prey and water, and so her choice of den sites had been restricted by the weather. Finally, Noorjahan was hemmed in by Noon and her two grown cubs and was thus not inclined to use the portion of the home range bordering and overlapping with Noon's. Quite simply Noorjahan had run out of site-options. These reasons combined to give us a unique observation.

A Predictable Routine

Until mid May, Noorjahan followed a remarkably predictable routine centred on the cubs in the cub caves. During most of the day, the cubs stayed in the cub caves. Sometimes Noorjahan would be resting in the tiger caves nearby perhaps an indication that young cubs can pester a tiger mother! However, it also indicated that she was not too worried about their security. Sometimes the cubs ventured out, one at a time. Just outside the cave, the lone cub would chew a stick and climb a branch unsteadily. If the wind blew a leaf or two, it would chase it, but not far. When all of them were out, which was not often, they would indulge in a little play. Within an area of about 30 square metres, they felt quite at ease. It was noticeable though that they usually sought cover even when playing. And they were jumpy. Perceiving any danger, real or imaginary, they would bolt unerringly back into the caves. Any loud noise, in particular, frightened them. It is doubtful whether they could see clearly and vehicle movement also guaranteed a quick disappearance. At around 4 p.m. they would be awake but inactive, faces near the mouth of the cave, sitting and waiting expectantly.

She unfailingly returned in the evenings, usually between 5.p.m. and 6 p.m. Usually, her arrival would be announced. A distant booming call of a sambar

Noorjahan places a firm paw on the cheek of a playful cub, her way of letting the youngster know that she is not interested in joining in their play. Sometimes Noorjahan snarled at her cubs when they tried to involve her in the fun. The message always got through.

An alert Noorjahan surrounded by her three playful cubs. The cubs at this age are totally dependent on their mother for protection - they have little idea what constitutes danger and have no means of defence or escape.

meant that she would be arriving in half an hour. A bark of a langur sitting on a tree overlooking the nala implied that she would materialize in only a few minutes. Sometimes it was Noorjahan herself who came roaring in. But occasionally, she would appear like a ghost, gliding her way through the nala noiselessly. Noorjahan always looked powerful, yet she moved softly.

Although she approached from various directions, she always stopped at the gorge rim to scan and assess the scene. Satisfied, she picked her way down and called, the cubs would perk up, ears twitching. As her calls came nearer, confirmation would dawn on the cubs as they bundled out of the cave and tried to pinpoint her position. The bolder male would scramble up, wait, scramble up, wait. By this time Noorjahan would have chosen her place and would guide the cubs to her by more vocalizations. Invariably the cubs would hurtle themselves at her, the bolder male first, ecstatic with joy at seeing her!

The first stage was an energetically affectionate greeting. The next stage involved leaping at Noorjahan's body. For a while Noorjahan was a gigantic toy as the cubs ran, jumped, slid and fell all over her. It was difficult not to be touched by such an uninhibited demonstration of happiness. Meanwhile

One of Noorjahan's cubs flings itself with affection at Noorjahan's head. The tiger mother is extremely tolerant when her cubs are this size.

Noorjahan licked and groomed any cub that strayed near her mouth. This was to stimulate blood circulation and by vigorously licking the genital region of the cub, the tigress also promoted urination and defecation. Then came feeding. The cubs had already established a teat order so that there was minimal argument. Each cub would work with a paw, in a circular fashion, to stimulate the flow of milk. Sometimes Noorjahan would roll over too soon, leaving one cub wanting more. It would cry and nuzzle her, pleading and yelping, until she relented and rolled back.

Feeding time over, the cubs would play and explore. Play would involve jumping on an unsuspecting sibling, chasing each other and climbing bushes. Noorjahan would also come in for some rough treatment. But, of course, she was in control. Some measured coughing and growling would sometimes work to stop a cub annoying her. If the play got too rough she would simply hold down the culprit under a massive paw. If, in its exploration, a cub wandered too far, Noorjahan would rise, pick up the intrepid explorer in her mouth, and carry it back to drop it unceremoniously where she wanted it to be. Noorjahan also took an active part in play, remaining seated all the time. Getting the cubs to chase, catch and bite her tail was a popular game. Another game involved

Noorjahan carrying one of her wayward cubs in her mouth. If, in exploration, a cub wandered too far, Noorjahan would rise, pick up the intrepid explorer, and carry it back to drop it unceremoniously where she wanted it to be.

Noorjahan holding her paw up for a cub to knock down. Since a tiger's paw can stun a 200 kg sambar, a cub had no chance of making any impression on it. Nevertheless, it would try its best.

Watching Noorjahan feed, tolerate, discipline, play with and generally take care of the cubs reminded us of watching a lioness in Africa do the same. We could see many similarities and no major differences, in the care lavished on the cubs by the world's two biggest cats. But it was the tenderness, above all, which was striking.

After dark we would have time to reflect and one subject we often wondered about was tigers and routines. It seems that for tigers, getting or supplying food is organized by routine. The character of the routine obviously varies with the composition and ages of the tiger family as well as features of the habitat and the season. It may be that having acquired a home range, a tigress will get into a routine which is efficient, given the environment. Nomadic tigresses may lack routines for acquiring food and, as a result, suffer from a loss of efficiency. This may be one factor contributing to the observation that nomadic tigresses are less healthy than those with home ranges.

Noorjahan often played with the cubs when they were at this age but some of the time it was in a passive manner. For example, she let the cubs regard her as a gigantic toy that they could bash at and play on.

Start of a New Phase

When the cubs were about eight weeks old, they began a new phase. We found their footprints alongside Noorjahan's, up to 500 metres from the cub caves. She had begun to take the cubs on walkabouts from the base. There then followed a major development. One evening, we saw the cubs waiting outside the caves until dark. Noorjahan had not turned up. In fact, she had killed opposite the forest rest house and led the cubs to the kill that night. There was also a fresher set of footprints leading from the kill to the cub caves; clearly the family had returned before dawn. So the cubs were now supplementing their diet with meat. Throughout that day, the cubs stayed in the cub caves and Noorjahan slept in the tiger caves. The next morning, we saw the family return to the caves at about 7.45 a.m. - the cubs had been out again. A couple of days later, we found drag marks of a chital kill which she had brought almost up to the cub caves, a distance of 750 metres. Clearly a new phase was setting in. By mid-May, it was becoming difficult to sight her. Her movements, partly because of the unbearable daytime heat, were now taking place at night. In the evening there was also the andhi - a hot, swirling

Brahminy Ducks breed in the desolate lake-studded areas of the Tibetan plateau but many migrate south to spend the winter in India. In Ranthambhore they seek out the clean, open stretches of the lakes.

wind raising dust and a few heavier objects as well, reducing visibility to almost zero - clearly not a good time to hunt.

Catching up with Noon and Her Cubs

While Noorjahan was thus occupied, what about her neighbour and mother, Noon? It may be recalled that Noon with her two cubs had moved out of the core area of the lakes, as Noorjahan began to occupy the area next to it. There was some overlap between the two home ranges and pug-marks of both tigresses were sometimes found not only in the common area but also in each other's home ranges. They seemed to be tolerant neighbours.

The core of Noon's home range was what is designated as Track 1, a monotonous route with dense vegetation on one side and thick woodland on the other. Light is poor and visibility low, but there is usually water here and enough prey for a tiger to subsist on. Noon's cubs, some 15 months older than Noorjahan's, were certainly looking healthy and growing steadily but they remained secretive. This may be due to the lack of traffic along Track 1. Once,

A migratory bird species, Common Teals are usually seen during winter in Ranthambhore. They are agile ducks and feed mainly on vegetable matter.

Noon killed a female sambar in the Tambakhan nala. This is a deep nala with good cover and poor light, so visibility is quite bad. The vehicle track cuts through one of the nala sides and the kill was about 70 meters down below. The noteworthy thing was that Noon was not at all concerned about the presence of tourist vehicles but the cubs certainly were. They were furtive and jittery, and when a few unthinking tourists got down from their vehicle to get a better look, the cubs fled to the top of the nala's other side.

Noon's Forays

For a week or so after Noon's Tambakhan kill the family stayed within her home range. Then she sprang a surprise. Noorjahan's cubs were about three weeks old and Noon called at the lakes with her two cubs. At about 1.30 p.m. she walked along the shore of Padam Talao opposite the Jogi Mahal forest rest house, into the tall, yellow grass some 300 metres away. At this time, Noorjahan was confining herself to a very tiny area around Jalra, only about 100 metres away. Noon's cubs were nonplussed by the people watching

A poignant retreat: Noon's two cubs walk along a shrunken Padam Lake, bathed in the warm evening light, following their mother some distance ahead.

excitedly from the rest house and the female cub nearly turned back. The cubs covered the last fifty metres of open terrain at a fast gallop. But cubs will be cubs and Noon's male cub could not resist charging from the cover and into the open, not once but twice. Both times the intended victim was a thirsty chital at a distance of 30-50 metres. Since Noon herself did not bother, it seemed that they were futile charges. Interestingly, after each charge the cub looked around, saw the watching public at the rest house, and immediately ran back to cover.

There was no contact made between Noon and Noorjahan this time, although they may have been aware of each other's presence. In the evening, Noon emerged from the cover and walked directly back the way she had come. It seemed that she had made up her mind to leave the area, at least for the time being. We watched with a twinge of sadness, the abducted queen of the lakes with her coat glistening gold in the low evening light, leading her cubs away from her former haunts. They paused once to drink but after that it was quick march, watched with bated breath by the sambar and the chital. Not a sound was made by the watching animals. Interestingly, Noon did not spray or claw a tree even once. It was a lovely evening walk, but really a poignant retreat.

In late April, Noon did return to the dam near Malik Talao - the portion of her home range which overlapped with that of Noorjahan and Laxmi. Incidentally, all three tigresses had cubs - Noon's were sixteen months old, Laxmi's were seven months old and Noorjahan's were almost two months old - and the ages of the cubs are a convincing piece of evidence that the tigers in Ranthambhore do not have a mating season. One reason why Noon is an interesting tigress is that she is always full of surprises. This time, she was lying in ambush directly beneath the dam wall. To view her, one had to get down from the jeep and bend to look directly below at the bottom of the vehicle wall which is only a few meters high. Noon would snarl at the peering face but would not budge. Presently three langurs came capering down the nala side and once at the bottom, started to move away from Noon. Once their backs were turned, she got up and crept quickly after them, using whatever cover was available. But the langurs kept moving and she ran out of cover. She had a go anyway and charged over a distance of 25 metres. She missed narrowly, scattering the langurs, all of whom took refuge in trees and barked incessant alarm calls. Like a tennis player who had narrowly missed an ace, Noon turned back, walking easily. She paused to drink from the pool, resumed her ambush position and then promptly went to sleep.

The next morning, Noon and her cubs were in the Malik-Lakarda Nala, in the core area of Laxmi's home range. From a height of about 200 meters, they could be seen on a kill on the nala bed. Even then, the cubs were wary. On seeing people out of vehicles, they immediately sought cover. It seemed likely that Noon had walked from the dam into the nala in search of prey. She had evidently successfully hunted in the night and had brought the cubs to the kill.

Two days later they were at the dam again. There was an unrecognizable carcass in the water and all three tigers were bulging, wet and muddy. By 8 a.m. they were heading for home, via Tambakhan nala, with Noon in the lead followed at a distance of twenty metres by her male cub and lastly the female cub keeping in cover and bringing up the rear. After that, the family were not seen outside the core of their home range till the end of the season.

So it appears that Noon did not come across Noorjahan's cubs. The long awaited meeting of the two families was to happen in the next season.

Taking Stock

The exciting 1989-1990 season drew to a close. But looking back, it was difficult to avoid noticing that the worrying trend in the disappearance of tigers was continuing. The season had included 3 puzzling vanishing acts. Noon's second cub from the first litter was absent. Adabalaji Female had gone, leaving only her daughter, now an adult and occupying her mother's home range. The disappearance of Bakola Ben's family was also complete with the vanishing of the tigress herself. The disappearance of these tigers cannot be taken lightly. This slow attrition was mystifying.

On the plus side, four tigresses in Ashoka's territory were successfully raising ten cubs. Together with the adults, that made a total of 15 tigers. It transpired, as Ashoka and Bhaiyu were consolidating their holds in their respective territories , that the take-over from Kublai and Daku was now a fact. But Ashoka was successfully building up his empire and it would be interesting to see how Bhaiyu would hold him in check. There was always the possibility of a new male arriving on the scene which could upset the social order. Tigresses breed well in peace and security, but males disputing territories cause disruption. Ashoka's tigresses were doing well, helped by the fact that his territory was in the heart of the tourist zone of the park where non-tourist disruptions were minimized. In contrast, all did not seem well further away in Bakola and beyond, and no births had been reported there. This was clearly food for thought.

Noorjahan with one of her cubs striding along the lake shore. The mother is leading her cubs to a kill but is in no hurry. She will pause to drink and to take in the surroundings.

The Dynasty Continues

TIGER ENCOUNTERS AT THE LAKES

The 1990-91 tiger viewing season began with a change at the helm: Ranthambhore had a new field director. In the country as a whole, there were also changes. The prime minister of India resigned in November 1990 and the new prime minister headed a very tenuous political alliance. The situation in the country was explosive: there were on-going, sometimes violent, religious conflicts, the Punjab independence movement was tinged with militancy, and the state of Kashmir was very tense. Against this volatile background, the resident tourists trimmed their travel plans. The overseas tourists to Ranthambhore decreased as well. Perhaps The Gulf War had a hand in this reduction. In addition, many Westerners were anticipating a recession, with the consequence that the demand for overseas holidays fell.

With the new appointment, the park management was initially galvanized into action. Patrolling to discourage wood and grass poachers as well as illegal cattle graziers, was intensified. There was some reshuffling of posts. Diesel jeeps, which make a racket, were banned from the park. Fees were hiked up to reduce tourist numbers (or was it to raise park revenue?). All the existing regulations affecting tourists, such as no off-track driving, adherence to park times and so on, were vigorously enforced. But all this furious activity lacked credibility since the ever-increasing number of VIP's escaped all regulations and continued to enjoy the park's amenities as well as the lavish hospitality of the park management, free of all charges and with extra privileges thrown in. Inevitably, patrolling of the park slackened. As usual, there was a lack of will and stamina. For experienced observers of the park's management, there was a distinct feeling of déjà vous.

More New Arrivals

In October 1990, the first big tiger event was the sighting of Nalghati Beti with two cubs, a male and a female, in Nalghati Valley. The cubs had probably been born in September and its hard to think of anyone but Ashoka siring them. From December, the family were seen every three days or so. The cubs became used to vehicles, although they retained some wariness. The great advantage of Nalghati valley to the tigers is that there is only one track which runs through it and the terrain on either side is not suitable for vehicles. So Nalghati Beti and the cubs could move away from the track whenever they chose to. Whenever she had the cubs with her she walked in cover on the valley bed whereas whenever she was alone she moved on the vehicle track.

In contrast to Nalghati Valley, Bakola appeared deserted during daylight hours; the tigers seemed to have reverted to their nocturnal habits. Every three weeks or so, a tiger would be sighted in the area but it would promptly run away upon being seen. So identification from facial markings was out of the question. However, the pug-marks indicated that there was one male and one female. Lakarda was also disappointing. Laxmi and her cubs appeared to have simply vanished; there were no pug-marks, let alone any sightings. Where had they gone? Alas, the park management wasn't interested in their whereabouts and arrogantly discouraged others from taking the initiative to search for the missing tigers.

In addition to Nalghati Valley, the areas of Sindwar and Adabalaji proved to be good for tiger viewing. Noon was in occupancy of Sindwar, which straddles the monotonous Track 1, and her female cub, nearly two years old in October, was digging in at the adjoining area of Adabalaji, which bestrides the main road to the park. Noon's male cub was unsettled, reflecting his age. He wandered at random between Adabalaji, Sindwar and the lakes.

Noorjahan sits spinx-like on an outcrop overlooking Malik Dam. From this vantage point she has a clear view of the animals coming in to drink at the dam.

Alive with Tigers

No area could match the lakes - this ecosystem was simply alive with tiger activity. Noorjahan's cubs had survived the hazards of the monsoon to reach an irrepressible stage in their lives. They had also grown to an impressive size; when viewed from a distance, any one of the seven month old cubs could sometimes be mistaken for an adult. So, not surprisingly, the outstanding feature of the 90-91 season at Ranthambhore was this tiger family. It turned out that during the first half of the season the cubs were just cubs, playful, curious and adorable. In the second half, however, they began to mature and acquire hunting skills. Noorjahan herself proved to be a capable mother, providing her cubs with food, comfort and protection. Ashoka, too, carried out the important paternal function of affording security. However, true to his character, he usually remained hovering in the background.

The picturesque lakes, then, were the setting in which these five tigers played out their roles. Noorjahan, now the undisputed queen of the lakes, varied her use of the home range with the seasons. From October to February, she made the area around Malik lake her base. During this winter period, there was good cover and plenty of prey which made it relatively easy for Noorjahan to hunt. She made catching wild boar her speciality, often bursting from cover on an unsuspecting pig.

From very early on, one of the two male cubs, we shall call him Bhimsen, began to stand out. The original Bhimsen is one of the five Pandav brothers in the Hindu epic of Mahabharata and the legendary figure is renowned for his size and strength. Likewise, Bhimsen the tiger cub was big and strong. He also capitalized on his size whenever the chance arose. Thus one morning Noorjahan charged from tall grass on a boar sow with young ones trotting by. She had, in fact, targeted the last piglet and caught it with ease. Noorjahan duly carried the piglet back into the grass where Bhimsen snatched it from her and ran away. He was very possessive and none of the others could share in the kill.

The resident prey animals in the Malik area began to anticipate Noorjahan and became more wary than usual. With many pairs of eyes and ears on the alert, she often surrendered the weapon of surprise. Communication among prey animals is surprisingly fast. A grazing chital looks up frequently and upon seeing a sambar, say, peering hard in to the thicket, joins in the surveillance. Within minutes, most nearby animals suspend their activities and try to pick out the suspected predator. So periodically, Noorjahan would change areas and she usually descended first to Rajbagh lake. Accordingly, one December morning we found the family on the move near Malik lake. The cubs were in the lead, perhaps because Noorjahan herself was pausing every now and then to scan for prey. It was remarkable the way the cubs could anticipate the direction their mother would take. Perhaps they had sensed that she was on the hunt and had learnt the route from one hunting spot to another. As the tigers moved through a lightly wooded area interspersed with open maidans, the cubs had many opportunities to explore, chase and play. They did crazy things like sitting on top of each other and climbing daunting trees. It is doubtful whether such activities helped their mother in her hunting.

We lost the family at mid-morning when the tigers casually slipped into the nala that cuts across the yellow grass-covered incline separating Rajbagh and Malik lakes. The nala has deep hollows where rain water collects and tends to remain. Prey animals come here to drink and so it is a fruitful place for a hungry tiger to lie in ambush. This kind of change in Noorjahan's hunting strategy - if looking actively for prey doesn't work let the prey come to you - was quite usual. On this occasion, however, she wasn't able to add to the bones littering the area. She left the cubs and made her way to Rajbagh lake below where, in the tall grass which can hide most sizable animals, she killed a chital. Characteristically, Noorjahan took her time before she climbed back, calling out to her cubs. The cubs, ever alert for signs of their mother immediately called in reply. Satisfied, Noorjahan settled down with a heavy sigh, halfway up the incline, and groomed herself assiduously. Predictably, the cubs emerged cautiously and then ran to Noorjahan with obvious relief. Upon reaching up to nuzzle their mother, they smelt meat and promptly went berserk, nuzzling and rubbing so that the tigers' bodies were intertwined in a sea of stripes. But Noorjahan could not be hurried. Taking her own time she led the cubs to Rajbagh lake. She naturally paused to drink on the way, unintentionally tormenting the cubs even further.

When the tigers were hidden in the grass, it was hard on the tourists. If lucky, peering through binoculars, they would catch a flicking tail. If very lucky, they would see the tigers emerge to drink from the lake before retiring to their hideout once again. Otherwise, all they could watch were crows waiting nearby and sometimes diving into the grass, and all they could hear were occasional loud growls. But the unexpected always happens when observing tigers and on this occasion we saw Ashoka who had come uninvited to share the kill. We saw all five of them together, sitting in the shallow waters of the lake, lit by the low angle of the sinking sun. Ashoka stayed for as long as the food lasted and then he went away. Where to next? Only he knew as he padded on with purpose in his every stride.

Ashoka's behaviour may appear inconsiderate, yet he was partly responsible for the breeding success of the tigresses in his home range. He patrolled and

A portrait of Noorjahan taken as she spots an unwary prey animal and commences a stalk.

marked his home range assiduously, thereby doing a good job of keeping strange male tigers out of his area. He was also continually adding to his home range and this must have kept him quite busy. Fortunately he had his tigresses to help him make his task less onerous. Thus, in that episode, after he had left Noorjahan and her cubs, he was next spotted in Nalghati Valley feeding on a sambar kill with Nalghati Beti and their two cubs.

It is thought as a rule that male tigers repel strange males from their home range but tolerate all females. The reasoning is that the male wants as many females as he can manage in his home range to enhance his breeding success. Thus Ashoka had Nalghati Beti, Noorjahan, Noon and Noon's daughter in one large section of his home range and Laxmi in another.

The Long-awaited Meeting

Noon continued to make her forays to the lakes area. Her two cubs were now over two years old and so the trio amounted to formidable muscle power. Were they a threat to Noorjahan and her cubs?

Noorjahan waits in ambush in the tall grass fringing Rajbagh Lake, watching an approaching small group of sambar deer with young. The tigress is very hungry but also very patient. She is prepared to wait for the prey to come within striking distance.

The chance to find out occurred on a cold but invigorating morning on the last day of the year. Noorjahan had killed a chital at Mori, (a collecting place for the water that overflows from Rajbagh lake to Padam lake during the monsoons) and by 6 a.m. had dragged it into the tall yellow grass. There were occasional glimpses of the feeding tigers whenever one of the cubs looked up, out of habit, to check out the surroundings. By 8 a.m. most of the kill had been devoured and the cubs started to walk about in the dry grass mosaic. Then, at about 9.15 a.m., the lull in activity was pierced by the unmistakable alarm call (rather like a veteran car horn) of sambar. About 15 minutes later Noon appeared on the crest of a small hill with her vibrant male cub in tow. With uncanny accuracy, she zoomed in on her daughter and family, prompting two of Noorjahan's cubs to scamper away to safety. Noon stopped 10 metres from Noorjahan who got up. Face to face, they stared at each other silently for a

minute. Bhimsen and Noon's cub were still, watching intently. Then Noon broke the stalemate by moving decisively away from her daughter. Noorjahan, taking the cue, moved quickly in the opposite direction towards her two cubs, with Bhimsen walking alongside her. They retired to the meadow where Noon, Noorjahan and her twin brother had hunted together years ago. Noon's male cub drew alongside his mother to watch his elder sister's retreat with interest, before turning to examine the remains of the kill. After a thorough investigation, Noon and son moved on. Noorjahan and the cubs remained in the meadow for some ten minutes. The cubs played a little, perhaps expressing relief, with Noorjahan disciplining them whenever they tried to involve her in the fun. Noon and Noorjahan appeared to tolerate each other; apparently they had no quarrel. Perhaps there was some sort of bond between mother and daughter that had survived. Noon's male cub was aware of his elder sister's offspring, but his attitude towards them was one of indifference. They posed no threat to him and he had no other motive for being aggressive. When Noorjahan moved off, it was with a noticeable limp. The next day, 1 January 1991, she moved no more than a few hundred metres, spending most of the day with her cubs, camouflaged in the tall grass fringing Rajbagh lake. She was waiting in ambush though, and focused sharply whenever there was a chance of a stray animal drifting into range. Hunting, however, was only a remote possibility with three cubs around since they were somewhat restive and often gave her position away, to the undisguised astonishment of the chital and the sambar. The cubs were still there the next morning but Noorjahan had apparently given them the slip. She had, in fact, made her way to the Malik area and there she waited at a vantage point overlooking Malik lake area and there she waited at a vantage point overlooking Malik anicut (or dam). She stayed there throughout the day, sitting sphinx-like, seemingly shackled to the lookout. At dusk she picked out a nilgai coming to drink and commenced a laborious stalk. It was agonizingly slow, her foot no doubt being too painful to use, and she gave up after inching forward ten metres. She had reached tall grass by then and there she spent the night.

Since the suspicious sambar have stopped well outside Noorjahan's reach, she commences on a careful stalk through the grass. As soon as she was spotted, she charged at the sambars, fleeing into the lake. But for an unexpected skid in the mud, she might well have caught one.

One doesn't really know how these things happen but Noorjahan's limp was no worse the next day and began improving the day after. On the fifth day she was putting her foot down confidently and walking properly again. Her activity perked up as well. On the sixth day she charged at some sambar in the waters of Padam lake. Unsuccessful, she moved to Rajbagh lake where she stalked a male sambar. When the stag moved away, she fixed her attention on a sambar hind and waited in ambush. The hind moved away also so Noorjahan had nothing to show for her efforts as the sun descended behind the hills. She looked fragile, but her limp had gone and she was back in action.

The tiger, like all big cats, lets hunger dictate its hunting effort. To begin with, after it has fed to the full, it does little else but sleep and drink. Even a couple of days can pass before it takes even a cursory interest in hunting again. But as time moves on, its interest increases and so does its efforts. If still unsuccessful, after the first four or five days, it can devote entire days to hunting. Thus it was with Noorjahan when, on the seventh morning, we picked her out moving between Padam and Rajbagh lakes. That she was in serious predatory mood was easy to infer from the way she kept on stopping to scan and the way she was studying the distant chital. It was in this manner that she spent the entire morning, moving from one hunting spot to another. She did rest in the fierce heat of the early afternoon, but by three p.m. she was on the move again. Moving purposefully along the shore of Rajbagh lake, she charged prematurely at a chital, perhaps out of frustration. The rush brought her to the tall grass at one corner of the lake and here she waited in ambush. When evening came, two male sambars passed within fifty metres of her. They had come to drink and also to feed on the water-plants of the lake. But she was biding her time. A small group of sambar hinds with young approached, and Noorjahan tensed. They came closer and stopped within 30 metres of the crouching tigress. She let a few minutes pass before commencing on a stalk through the tall grass. The stalk changed to a charge when the sambars' suspicions were confirmed. Her rush was full-blooded and although she skidded momentarily in the mud, she regained her balance almost at once and continued her sprint right into the lake, her eyes fixed on the fleeing deer. She missed though, but for the slip she wouldn't have been climbing slowly out of the water on the far shore looking distinctly rueful to the sound of disorderly sambar calls.

The end to Noorjahan's trials was something of an anti-climax. Very early the next morning, she appeared dragging a sambar baby through the grass fringing Rajbagh lake. It was the eighth day and her ordeal was over. For sure enough as the rest of the winter wore on, she managed as competently as before, with the result that her cubs continued to grow.

Noorjahan veiled by tall, yellow grass. Such grass at the edge of the lakes camouflages the tiger, enabling it to hide, feed without disturbance, and stalk prey.

Noorjahan makes an appearance, dragging a sambar baby through the tall, yellow grass fringing Rajbagh Lake. Despite their reputation as efficient predators, tigers have to work hard to make a living. Even when the game is abundant, they may have to go for several days without a large kill.

The Trials of Noorjahan

A TIGRESS STRUGGLES TO RAISE HER THREE CUBS

Although it is only Spring, the areas of water have diminshed considerably. In fact, Malik lake is reduced to a couple of tiny pools of water. A vast distance separates these from the grass-fringed shore. Large gaps have also appeared in the grassy border and through these herbivores amble leisurely to drink at the shrunken pools. Clearly, a tiger would have trouble stalking prey. However, Rajbagh and Padam lakes still have respectable stretches of water which are attracting the chital and the sambar. Here, the deer are congregating to form sizeable herds. Present too, although not in plentiful numbers, are the antelopes - nilgai and chinkara. The latter is a gazelle, similar to the dainty Thomson's gazelle. Unlike its African cousin however, the chinkara is solitary and elusive. Langur babies are also numerous, clinging tightly to their mothers. Wild boar piglets can be readily spotted, trotting military style behind a finicky sow. And at almost every corner there is a strutting peacock, displaying his wares to apparently disinterested peahens.

Functioning in harmony with the season, Noorjahan has moved out of the Malik lake area to base herself at Rajbagh lake. From here she also undertakes frequent hunting forays to Padam lake. Along the swampy far shore of Padam lake, there is a fringe of dense tall grass. The grass is various shades of yellow, making it difficult, at least for human eyes, to pick out a striped predator waiting in ambush.

It is warmer than usual for this time of year. Even the dawn breeze blowing over Padam lake feels warm. In the afternoon Bhimsen and Nakul, his brother, are spotted panting laboriously under the shade of a large tree and in the cool of evening they take to sitting in exposed stretches of water.

A Daunting Task

Spring found Noorjahan facing a somewhat daunting task. Her three cubs, nearly a year old, could not kill anything sizable and so were quite helpless on their own. They compounded the pressure on her to hunt by sometimes spoiling her hunting attempts, unintentionally of course. Bhimsen was the biggest culprit. Once, Noorjahan spotted a chital in a promising position. She instinctively lowered herself out of its direct sight. The cubs did the same. But, after a while, Bhimsen couldn't resist a peep and so raised his head. Noorjahan let out a barely audible growl whereupon a chastened Bhimsen promptly lowered himself. But, predictably, after another short interval, the head was bobbing up again. Noorjahan reprimanded him yet again and this process was repeated several times until the chital took fright and darted away.

On the Hunt

You could never tell when Noorjahan was under pressure. She never looked harassed, indeed, she was always the picture of implacability. Tigers seem to have a relaxed air about them even when concentrating hard. Noorjahan did hunt on her own quite often. The broad pattern of her solo hunting excursion was to move from one hunting spot to another, spending some time at each location. Occasionally, she was able to catch something while moving between locations. Thus on the 3rd April, on her way to the masjid sited between Padam and Rajbagh lakes, she spotted a chital grazing with its back towards her. By creeping expertly, she narrowed the distance but a stretch of open ground remained. It was a tricky situation and Noorjahan decided to wait in concealment. After a while, the driver of a huge canter (truck) waiting in anticipation nearby, started the engine, thereby momentarily diverting the chital's attention. Noorjahan seized the chance. First she crept forward a few metres, lizard style, and then charged. The stag ran for its life as soon as it

As Noorjahan applies the killing bite, the chital's tongue hangs out and its glazed eyes widen. While she was carrying out this attack, Noorjahan was visibly trembling. She held her firm grip until the chital was dead and then dragged the carcass into cover before setting off to fetch her cubs.

A male nilgai, often called a 'blue bull'. The nilgai is the largest antelope native to Asia. Although it looks ungainly, the nilgai is quite speedy. Female nilgai and their calves however are frequent targets of tiger attacks.

The chinkara or Indian gazelle is a small, graceful animal found in small numbers in Ranthambhore. Unlike its African cousin, the Thomson's gazelle, it is shy and elusive.

noticed the hurtling tigress, but it was too late. Noorjahan, leaping after him, pounced on the chital. Through the settling dust, she could be seen dragging the stag across the track and on to the incline. She stopped halfway and sat down to complete the suffocation. The chital's tongue hung out and its glazed eyes widened. Blood from its neck began to show. Noorjahan was trembling visibly but her throat grip was tight and firm. The chital twitched spasmodically as its life drained away. Noorjahan took her time and made sure. Then, having completed the strangulation, she dragged her kill into the tall grass fringing Padam lake. There she rested for half an hour before walking along the shore to find her brood. The cubs greeted her with obvious delight, milling around her. They were quick to smell the feast on Noorjahan's face and were impatient to commence feeding. But she was, characteristically, in no hurry to lead them back to the kill. She walked, stopped, laid down, played, rolled over and, in such tiger fashion, slowly led the cubs to the stag.

Noorjahan had a special hunting technique in her repertoire. Twice we observed her attempting to first cut the prey off by running ahead in a wide detour and then waiting in ambush for the unsuspecting animal. However, the first attempt resulted in failure because a jeep load of tourists almost ran her over as they attempted to get ahead of the sambar at the same time. But the second time she caught a chital neatly as it walked unawares into the trap she had sprung. She dragged the chital a short distance and then rested awhile before setting out to look for her cubs.

Noorjahan invariably reacted very fast to any opportunities that arose and this ability paid off repeatedly. She once spotted another unfortunate chital, grazing in the forest, unaware of the danger. Noorjahan froze in mid-stride for a fraction of a second and then charged straight into the forest, a distance of fifty metres. Two minutes later, we found her sitting on her hind legs, suffocating the deer.

Whenever Noorjahan was thus occupied, the cubs had a lot of time to themselves. Much of this was spent just waiting for Noorjahan.

A strutting peacock displaying his wares to apparently disinterested peahens. Peafowl are found in their thousands in Ranthambhore. In studies carried out elsewhere, they were found to constitute the largest proportion of a tiger's diet.

A langur babe tightly clinging to its mother. Although the mother herself is exceptionally caring of her infant, females within a troop share the task of looking after the young for the first few weeks.

Bhimsen

Bhimsen was discernibly bigger and stronger than the other two cubs. He was about two and a half times the size of an adult male leopard and, in a chance encounter, a leopard would undoubtedly have taken flight without hesitation. Bhimsen was also bolder and more adventurous than the other two. Not surprisingly, his boldness, strength and inquisitive nature made him a natural leader. Nakul, in fact, followed him everywhere; it was as if Bhimsen was making all the decisions for him. With the two males paired, Sharmeelee, the female cub, was often found resting apart from her brothers. True to her name, she was shy. She was also very close to her mother, so that, whenever the foursome were on a walk together, she and Noorjahan often brought up the rear, walking contentedly side by side, with Bhimsen in the lead and Nakul tracking him.

When the cubs were on their own, Bhimsen sometimes wandered off. The other two might follow some distance behind, as if pulled by a force they had no inclination to resist. This was reminiscent of a cheetah mother being followed doggedly by her cubs. Once, when Bhimsen was rambling through a marshy portion of Padam lake, he spotted a baby crocodile, a metre long in length, resting in a shallow pool of water. He pounced like a flash and yanked it out. He then followed this instinctive action by taking his prize into tall grass to investigate it at leisure. By the time Nakul and Sharmeelee arrived, Bhimsen was deep in the grass. Nakul and Sharmeelee drank, sat and almost dozed off. After ten minutes they noticed that Bhimsen was up to something. As if on cue, they stalked up to and then jumped on him. The three got involved in a mad game of chase and the baby crocodile was forgotten.

Bhimsen also developed a habit of chasing sambar. He was quite indiscriminate about this - small, large, solo or a herd - as long as they were sambar. Very occasionally he inflicted this form of terror on other animals too, but sambar were manifestly his preferred target. Was Bhimsen succumbing to a basic instinct or was this an idiosyncratic characteristic?

Bhimsen, not surprisingly, was also the most self-assured cub in the presence of tourist jeeps. If only two or three vehicles arrived and kept their distance, the young tigers would merely turn their heads for a cursory glance. But eventually Bhimsen would stir into action and advance to sit nearer the jeeps with Nakul and Sharmeelee looking on with lukewarm interest. Sometimes he would walk right up to a jeep to examine it more thoroughly. This examination would include sniffing and also chewing anything rubbery. If there were too many jeeps or a vehicle came too close, the cubs would withdraw to a secluded place.

Into the Second Year

The cubs were about a year old now and sometimes Noorjahan would absent herself for two to three days, hunting or resting. We left her one evening, sleeping near Rajbagh lake. Driving along the shore of the lake, we came across a sambar baby whose front leg had been bitten off, probably by a crocodile. As it hobbled bravely, casting nervous glances in all directions, all the innocence of the young and the weak seemed embodied in those looks. Other sambar grazing nearby watched helplessly too. The baby, balancing itself on three legs, tried to nibble at the grass but it soon gave up the unequal struggle and lay down, a picture of calm resignation. There does appear to be considerable pain and hardship involved in living in the natural world.

Early next morning, there was Noorjahan, barely visible in the tall yellow grass, with crows perched in attendance in a nearby tree. She stayed put for a couple of hours, making us wonder if she intended to have the kill all to herself. But Noorjahan proved to be a dutiful mother for when she emerged with the crippled sambar baby it was intact. She half-dragged, half-carried it to Rajbagh Palace.

If Noorjahan made a kill further away, she first moved it to deep cover and then fetched the cubs. And whenever the kill was a large one, she would interrupt their feeding by taking them to water. On one occasion, after feeding for a while on a large sambar, she led the two smaller cubs to a small pool of water, a couple of kilometres away. (Bhimsen was extra-hungry and stayed to feed.) Sharmeelee and Nakul, unlike their mother, went through the preliminary ritual of snarling at the water in the pool. This presumably warns any crocodiles to keep away. Although the morning was quite cool, the tigers proceeded to immerse their bodies in the water, entering the pool backwards and keeping their heads clear of water. For about ten minutes, they sat there drinking now and then. It is strange, this love tigers have for water. Perhaps there is an evolutionary explanation. Tigers, having originated from a cold region, may possess an internal body-heating system still 'set' for low temperatures. Over the coming millenia evolution may reset the internal thermostat. In the meantime, even on cold winter mornings in India, tigers stay in the shade, avoiding direct sunlight.

After demolishing a large kill, the family tended to keep together awhile. Initially the tigers would spend most of the time resting, with occasional saunters for exercise or drink. Gradually, however, Noorjahan would become more purposeful during a walk, marking her home range - something that Bhimsen took to doing as well - and regarding prey animals with mild interest. The cubs would try to keep up with her and Noorjahan would often wait for them to catch up with her. But if, in due course, nothing chanced her way, Noorjahan would try to separate herself from the cubs. This might involve snarling at one that came too close to her. They still managed to tag along for a while though. Even with the cubs dogging her, Noorjahan was able to seize half-chances that sometimes occurred. If the animal caught was small, Bhimsen usually appropriated most of it but he did not always have things his own way. Early one morning in late April as the tigers were crossing from Padam lake to Rajbagh lake, Bhimsen wandered off by himself and accidentally spooked a chital hind and her fawn straight into Noorjahan's intended path. The tigress reacted instantaneously, exploding into an impressive sprint. In reacting to the fawn's mournful cry, Sharmeelee was a split second faster than Bhimsen. Noorjahan left the fawn for her daughter who seemed unusually determined to keep possession of it. When Bhimsen and Nakul approached Sharmeelee, she gave out warning growls before bounding away with the fawn dangling from her jaws. She disappeared into cover where, exploiting her advantage, she guarded her prize most effectively. She snarled fiercely when her brothers hesitantly approached, causing them to halt indecisively. Finally, the males sat down and cast longing glances at the little tigress. However, like leopard cubs, they had resigned themselves to the convention of finders keepers although they did approach Noorjahan, nuzzling her and whining. But she was indifferent to their pleas.

The hunt itself may be viewed as a co-operative effort, although Bhimsen had not spooked the chital intentionally. However, from winter onwards, there were instances of intentional co-operative hunting. Once, in January, watched by Noorjahan, the three cubs had begun a pincer movement in order to surround

Noorjahan dragging a heavy chital stag through a lightly wooded area. The strength of the tiger is legendary: folklore tells of a tiger leaping village compound walls with a domestic buffalo in its jaws.

Noorjahan's excited cubs rush to greet her when she appears after an absence of several hours. The hungry cubs can smell fresh meat when nuzzling their mother and this triggers frenzied activity.

a chital fawn near Malik lake. After they had overpowered it, Noorjahan had taken charge. Then, on the 20th March, the cubs revealed a new hunting style. Bhimsen, in the lead as usual, spotted an adult sambar at Rajbagh lake. He froze while Nakul and Sharmeelee crept wide of him and got into position. When Bhimsen initiated the chase, they sprinted too, perhaps in the hope that the sambar might run across and into their path. It didn't and Bhimsen couldn't close the gap either. Two weeks later, the family were walking along the dirt track through the forest when they spotted a sambar. The cubs immediately slipped into the forest whereas Noorjahan raced ahead on the track and then cut into the thicket. She missed narrowly, causing the panic stricken sambar to run crashing through the forest for half a kilometre. On 14th April, the staff of the forest rest house saw the three cubs chase a small herd of chital along the far shore of Padam Lake. From where she had positioned herself in the grass, Noorjahan pounced and caught one of the fleeing deer.

A Spinal Wound

The cubs were eager to learn to hunt but still dependent on Noorjahan. Early on the morning of 22nd April, Noorjahan was walking fast along the far shore of Padam lake. After 500 metres, she entered the water to sit in a favourite spot, but unusually she did not drink. When she resumed her brisk walk we noticed that she was twitching her tail frequently. Much to the relief of the alerted deer, she showed no inclination to hunt. When we had a better view, we saw an unusual wound at the base of her spine, just above her tail. It was round, narrow and very deep, as if something small but powerful had penetrated the spot. Was she in great pain? Had she sat in the water to soothe the wound? Was her manner of walking an attempt to keep the flies off? She entered the deep, cool nala at the mouth of Nalghati Valley and did not re-appear that day or the next. The cubs, in a secluded spot near Padam lake, were also inactive. At 6.00 p.m. on the second day, alarm calls signposted her path over the shoulder of Nalghati Valley and the descent to Rajbagh lake. She made straight for the water and submerged her entire body leaving only her head sticking out. Even as we left at dusk, she stayed in that tragi-comic pose.

On the third day Noorjahan put in a brief appearance with the cubs. But there was an air of despondency hanging over the family. Noorjahan's wound was getting worse - bleeding more and with some whitish substance inside. She was twitching her tail continuously and kept sniffing the air. She attempted to lick the wound, but couldn't quite reach it with her tongue. The entire family was looking lean but Noorjahan had lost all interest in hunting. Later on that morning, she went straight from Padam lake to Rajbagh Palace, alone, and stayed there, out of sight, throughout the day. For their part, the hapless cubs stayed rooted to a secluded spot at Padam lake.

A turning point in natural healing is hard to pinpoint. Perhaps recovery ensued when she appeared plastered in mud. But from that day on, she took to rolling in mud and began to take an interest in hunting. In due course, the wound healed completely, she was back in action and family life was secure once more.

Noorjahan drags a crippled sambar baby into a dense thicket, next to Rajbagh Lake, and thence onto the ruins of Rajbagh Palace. She carried the baby most of the time, pausing only twice to get her breath back

Noorjahan snarling at a nonplussed Bhimsen. Whenever Noorjahan wanted her private space she discouraged the cubs from coming too close to her by grimacing. Reluctantly, the cubs would settle down some distance away.

A Male Visitor

Throughout the cubs' development, Ashoka had been unobtrusively keeping an eye on the territory and providing the family security. Typically, he was sometimes glimpsed for a minute and then lost from view. But now and then, one did manage to obtain an audience with him for a longer period. Thus one morning we picked him out, moving briskly up the incline above Rajbagh lake. A jackal spotted him from afar, ran across, and distracted a few chital who had not yet sighted Ashoka. The tiger took his chance, sprinting and then pouncing on a straggler, within a matter of seconds. He bit through the chital's neck and then dragged it behind a log, devouring it rapidly. Ashoka then sauntered down to Rajbagh lake and started to enjoy a dip, in the cool water. However, he was quick to get up and walk away when a jeep arrived on the scene. At the same time, on another day, Ashoka was walking to Padam lake when he quickened his pace, bent down, and pulled up a hare, holding it high as he surveyed the scene. He then carried the prize for several hundred metres before inexplicably dropping it, uneaten. Observations such as these were too few and far between to draw any conclusions about Ashoka's hunting style. However, to us he epitomised the supreme opportunist.

One male tiger did slip through to the lakes and stayed on for a couple of days. Perhaps Ashoka was elsewhere then. More likely it was further evidence that Ashoka was, indeed, the father of Noon's male cub. For it was him we saw feeding in the tall grass of Rajbagh lake one spring morning. As soon as he had finished eating, he started walking quickly, keeping a wary eye on us. When a jeep drove in, head on, he promptly changed course and headed for the deep Kukraj nala. He did not appear fully accustomed to vehicles. He stayed on around the lakes for another day and then disappeared.

May and June were hot, boiling hot, and there was also the andhi - a forceful, hot, dry wind that creates duststorms which blot out the landscape - to contend with. Noorjahan and her cubs kept a low profile and it seemed as if the tiger-viewing season would end uneventfully. However, one day in June, Noorjahan left the park and killed a domestic buffalo near a farm. She dutifully took her cubs to the carcass and the news of four tigers on a kill spread like wildfire amongst the local people. For three days the tigers feasted and the villagers also gorged themselves on this rare spectacle. It was all good fun for everyone concerned, except the buffalo and its owner. However, the close proximity of humans on foot to tigers accustomed to humans in vehicles, was a little worrying. But on this occasion, Noorjahan and her trio returned safely to the park and the villagers duly went back to their interrupted daily grind.

The monsoon rains came with a vengeance, quickly flooding the tracks, and the park closed down for tiger-viewing. The cubs were then just over 15 months old and still growing fast. They would be a year and a half old at the beginning of the next season and on the threshold of independence. That would be something exciting to look forward to.

Noorjahan and two of her cubs cooling off in the nearest pool of water she could find, after having finished feeding. For about ten minutes the tigers enjoyed the soak, lapping water now and then. But as the sun rose, she initiated a move towards the shady forest.

Despair & Hope

Ranthambhore tigers in a desperate struggle for survival

There was the most dismal of all starts to the October 1991 - June 1992 tiger-viewing season. Before Christmas, three topics dominated the gloomy conversations: the generally abysmal tiger sightings, the whereabouts of Bhimsen, Nakul, Sharmelee and Nalghati Beti's cubs, and the sad death of Badiya, the long-serving tiger-tracking master.

The tiger census of May 1991 had yielded a figure of 45 tigers, yet over the three months of October to December only nine different tigers were seen and then only intermittently. What could be the reason for this big drop in tiger sightings? The monsoon rains had been abundant. The rains had produced luxuriant cover, making it difficult to spot animals. If, in such circumstances, tigers choose not to show themselves there is little chance of finding them. But what was puzzling was the conspicuous absence of pug-marks. The prey animals were also difficult to locate in the lower reaches of the park. Strangely, even the hills were devoid of deer and antelope. Where could the herbivores be? Instead of wild animals there was a marked presence of cattle and their minders, grass-gatherers and wood-cutters. So although there was activity in the forest, Ranthambhore appeared tiger free. As if to emphasis the point, when the humans left at evening time, the forest became eerily quiet. The roar of the tiger was missing.

On the evening of the 4th of December, Badiya, a poverty-stricken and friendly forest tracker, had set out to buy food for his family in Sawai Madhopur. But instead of returning to his family he was found dead near the railway tracks, a few kilometres away from the town. Many questions were raised: was it an accident, suicide or murder? The air buzzed with these questions. Badiya was an honest and simple man, dedicated to the tigers of Ranthambhore. His death deeply moved people.

Where are the Tigers?

Were any of the tigers that we had been accustomed to seeing still around? Sadly, Laxmi was nowhere to be seen. To be sure, in October there was a fluke sighting of a tigress walking from Semli Valley to Lakarda; it might have been Laxmi. However, not a single tigress was subsequently seen in the Semli-Lakarda area throughout the season. Most knowledgeable people believed that Laxmi was dead. If true, something extremely precious had been lost. It is with a pang of sadness that one thinks of the cool, tolerant and trusting Laxmi, walking her domain leisurely with boisterous cubs in tow, simply engrossed in the daily business of living.

Noon, younger sister of Laxmi and at least as famous, also appeared to have vanished. A tigress resembling Noon was once seen on Track 1, far from the lakes. If it was Noon then the mighty tigress of the lakes had been relegated to the park's fringes. But that was the only sighting of her. The question as to Noon's whereabouts was raised in the state parliament so the park authorities had to take the matter seriously. Their response, however, was feeble. A man who ran a makeshift tea stall and who had no previous experience of tiger-tracking was hired to track tigers in place of Badiya. In fact, the forest department quickly established a motley gang of four trackers, inexperienced in the ways of the forest and inaccurate in their reading of clues in the wild. Once the minor storm over Noon had blown over, the park management lost interest in her and returned to the vital task of pampering VIPs.

Noorjahan waits on a forest track for her cubs to catch up with her. The forest which is the main habitat of the tiger has largely disappeared from Southern Asia. Deforestation has been brought about primarily by the expanding human population and a greater need for crops, firewood and domestic livestock.

A female nilgai striding across a clearing on a misty Ranthambhore morning. Nilgai are the largest native antelope of Asia and in a single game drive in Ranthambhore one can sometimes see antelope, gazelle and deer.

Noon must have been seen by more people than any other tiger in Ranthambhore. Like Laxmi she was tolerant and trusting. Tigers are like that, once they trust you, they ignore you and often drop their guard, sometimes falling asleep right in front of you.

Bhaiyu, Laxmi's male cub, now six years old, was finally sighted in Bakola in March. He appeared jumpy. On the few subsequent occasions when he was spotted, he kept to the shadows. Judging by a study of the footprints in and near Bakola, he was usually active at night. Bela, too, was around but like Bhaiyu, proved elusive.

Ashoka was also becoming shyer. He was still around though, for his pug-marks were all over his vast home range. His area took in Guda, Nalghati Valley, the Lakes, Lakarda and Track 1. At the place where Track 1 met the main road to the park, Ashoka entered the home range of Noon's female cub, Sindwar Female. She was three years old, petite in physique, but sexually mature. She and Ashoka provided the only noteworthy tiger event observed that winter. From the 22nd December to Christmas Ashoka was in close attendance to Sindwar Female and once, at the crack of dawn, was seen attempting to mate with her. It came to nothing since Sindwar Female came into heat again in February and, once again, Ashoka materialized to court her.

Nalghati Valley seemed bereft of tigers that winter although Nalghati Beti was present, minus the cubs. The youngsters had passed away in tragic circumstances. Sometime in May 1991, Nalghati Beti had been heard calling repeatedly in Nalghati Valley. She appeared agitated and paced restlessly, returning to a disused, empty well. There, at the bottom, cowering and meowing, were her two cubs. It's baffling how they got there. They may have been playing in the vicinity of the well, got carried away, and fallen in accidentally. The park management dropped meat and water down to them and later lowered a wooden contraption for the cubs to clamber out. They looked emaciated. Strangely, Nalghati Beti distanced herself from the cubs and, in their preoccupation with the VIPs, the park management neglected to keep an eye on them. They were never seen again.

Nalghati Beti herself was seen a number of times in the spring. On the morning of the 22nd March she was spotted waiting in ambush and in due course a few unknowing sambar walked into her trap. She timed her charge well, causing the deer to run frantically to escape. Twisting and turning in hot pursuit, she followed her victim behind a steep incline. There was a mournful cry and, after a pregnant pause, the faint rustle of a carcass being dragged along the ground.

At the lakes, although Noorjahan was seen, her three cubs could not be traced. Day after day, tourists searched in vain for the trio. It took time for their disappearance to sink in. But is it really possible for three grown cubs to simply vanish without leaving any clues whatsoever? It was all very puzzling. With the cubs gone and Noorjahan herself seen only occasionally, the lakes were empty of excitement. There was a sense of anti-climax.

The Search for Reasons

How can one account for these abysmal tiger sightings? To begin with, 800 millimetres of rain, a very high figure, had fallen during the monsoons. With water everywhere, prey animals were scattered, so the tigers were bound to be dispersed as well. Moreover, there was luxuriant cover, making tiger spotting more challenging. To compound the effects of rain, there were villagers and their cattle. They entered the park daily and Track 4 became notorious for its sightings of cattle. These incursions, which continued unchecked up to April, were bound to have an effect on the diurnal movements of the wary and cautious tiger.

So, there were plausible reasons for the decline in tiger visibility. Yet there were three awkward questions. Where were the tiger pug-marks? When one drove far and wide without seeing a single pug-mark, one began to wonder. There had been, admittedly, occasions in the past when one saw few tigers but one did see lots of pugmarks. The other puzzle was the absence of alarm calls. Much of the time the forest was unusually silent, save for the calling of birds. The final puzzle was an increase in leopard sightings. Past experience of Ranthambhore suggests that as the tiger population increases, leopards get displaced. This is because a tiger is intolerant of other predators like leopards and with its greater strength - a tiger is four times heavier than a leopard - is able to drive the spotted cat away. The return of the leopards was further evidence of the absence of many tigers from the park.

Concern for the park's tigers increased when a prediction failed to materialize. In Ranthambhore, when warmer weather sets in towards the end of February, water in the peripheral areas begins to evaporate and the herbivores get drawn into stretches of more permanent water, such as Padam and Rajbagh lakes. Sure enough, with increasing warmth, sightings of deer and antelopes grew steadily although it was a little disconcerting to note that the numbers were significantly down on previous years (in fact, all over the park, prey density appeared to be lower). With the hot weather, cover also began to wither away and the encroachment by villagers decreased as well. Things pointed to a sizeable increase in tiger sightings but the actual real increase was far too small and very disappointing. Ominously, leopard sightings went up dramatically.

A marked feature of herbivore behaviour during the spring was their relaxed demeanour. Every day it was almost as if one was watching a herd of cattle grazing in an exotic field. Nilgai nonchalantly plucked at tufts of grass. Sambar lounged about, watching contentedly as vehicles drove past. Chital, who are more jumpy than Sambar, moved about leisurely in tall grass as if they had been accustomed to grazing in that manner all their lives. The deer and the antelopes were obviously at ease where the tigers used to roam.

Clearly, the time had come to seek other explanations. One unpalatable possibility suggested itself dramatically when Badiya, the forest tracker, was found dead. There were many loose ends concerning the cause of Badiya's death and, inevitably, there was suspicion of foul play in the air.

The tranquil atmosphere of Ranthambhore had for some time been spoilt with stories of poaching and Badiya was reportedly unhappy before his death. Rumours circulating after the tracker's death said that he had witnessed tiger poaching and had been offered bribes to keep quiet. When he had refused, he had been threatened. But in India's caste system Badiya was a poverty-stricken harijan or 'untouchable' and was therefore of no consequence. Hence he could not command an audience. So he sought transfer to another park. But effecting the transfer quickly was no easy task for a man of his social status and the man who could not bear to see animals destroyed before his own eyes was killed. However, his death did serve one purpose: it brought the question of tiger poaching out into the open.

Chital mating in early morning light in Ranthambhore. The park is an excellent place in which to observe the behaviour of this dainty deer. The terrain in Ranthambhore is more open than elsewhere in Indian forests and the deer have grown accustomed to the presence of vehicles.

At the main police station at Sawai Madhopur, the Senior Officer recalled that on the night of the 29-30 December 1991 between 2 and 3 a.m., the police stopped a jeep which they suspected was carrying illicit liquor. In fact, the jeep was found carrying three recently shot chinkara. Kanjar tribesmen driving the jeep alleged that the antelopes had been shot at Devpura village outside the National park. The park management admitted that the poaching of animals such as chinkara, chital, sambar and hare did take place occasionally, on a small scale and for food consumption only. But regrettably, if this was possible, then so was tiger poaching.

Earlier in the year, acting on a tip-off, the park personnel made a swoop on Mansarovar Lake in Ranthambhore where they apprehended a few people from the city of Jaipur, 170 km away. The men alleged that they were picnicking. Yet they had rifles and rounds of ammunition with them. Their jeeps were seized and the men themselves were taken into custody, though later released on bail. The reason for relating this incident is that the remote parts of Ranthambhore are not under vigilance and people in fast-moving vehicles can enter and exit at will. Moreover, many parts of the park are easy to enter and leave easily at certain times. The general lack of vigilance means that Ranthambhore tigers are sitting targets for would-be poachers.

The Jigsaw Becomes Complete

With hindsight it is all too easy to see how the pieces of the trap came together - how the Ranthambhore tigers came to face a potentially fatal threat. From the mid-70s to the mid-80s, the tigers had been successfully insulated from disturbance by villagers and from murder by poachers. The park was well-protected: there was regular patrolling, even at night. Suspicious incidents were quickly investigated. The tigers thrived. Then came the tourists and the tigers became accustomed to human observers in four-wheeled vehicles.

Tourists in jeeps also provide excellent vigilance. But unfortunately, from the point of view of surveillance, tourists were constrained in their movements. Up to June 1988 the Bakola area's tigers thrived, save for the mysterious loss of one cub. Sometimes one could see four tigers within an area of two square kilometres. But when the park management closed Bakola to tourists (for the benefit of the VIPs of course) tiger-sightings in Bakola plummeted. Moreover, the park management's patrolling of the area was so lax that villagers quickly moved in, bringing their domestic animals with them. Perhaps they were not the only ones. Adult tigers are quite elusive, however, and manage to avoid human beings most of the time. They tend to stay under cover and frequent inaccessible areas. Laxmi, typically, had the ability to live in forbidding nalas, unseen and undisturbed. In fact, when unaccompanied by cubs, she could stay out of sight for weeks on end, simply by abandoning the use of open areas and functioning in secluded zones. If leopards are phantoms then tigers are ghosts.

No, the really vulnerable tigers are the habituated cubs; they are too trusting, and drawn into the open by a mixture of innocence and curiosity. They thus have a poor sense of danger. Also, since they don't hunt, they have one less reason to seek cover and of course, they are unskilled in the use of camouflage and stealth. So when sighted they tend to stay in the open. Inadvertently, cubs also tend to bring their mothers and sometimes their fathers out into view. Clearly, tiger families need greater protection than lone adults from hostile humans at least until the cubs have learnt the ways of adults. It is in the provision of this protection that the park authorities appear to have failed. There were some horrifying symptoms of general mismanagement in this area. Villagers moved in and out of the park at will: they were openly and fearlessly defiant. Once, the villagers threatened to set fire to the park if stopped and, in fact, on the 2nd March 1992 did so, burning off vast sections of the core area. The point is this: anyone with daring and defiance could move in and out of the park without real confrontation. The holes in the park's protection cover were huge. It is conceivable that when, during the monsoons, the tourists stopped visiting the park, the tigers, with cubs in particular, became sitting ducks for poachers.

Bad to Worse

The 1992 Tiger Census at Ranthambhore, whose results were awaited with trepidation, was carried out over the period of the 16th to 24th May. Alas, our worst fears were realized, for the number of tigers was down from the 1991 figure of 45 to only 17, a truly shameful revelation. Moreover all 17 tigers were reckoned to be in the core area, none in the fringes. The census confirmed the fate of many beloved tigers and, not surprisingly, there was an immediate hue and cry. The forest officials, having conducted the census, proclaimed that it was incorrect. Perhaps a cover-up was in the offing? But the local police, much to the shame of the forest department, took to patrolling the Park, and on the 24th June caught a poacher with a tiger skin. He confessed to having shot the tiger at point blank range after trapping it. He also admitted to having killed eight tigers and six leopards in the past three years.

In fact, since 1989, at least 20 tigers are feared to have been killed in Ranthambhore by gangs of poachers. The poaching route probably went something like this. From Ranthambhore, the skins and bones were sent out by railway parcel to Delhi and other places, marked as old clothes, plastic shoes and toys. The tiger body parts found their way to Nepal and then on to China, Taiwan, South Korea and Hong Kong. In the past China had slaughtered thousands of its own tigers and the massacre had created a temporary glut of tiger bones. The stockpile had satisfied demand for traditional Chinese medicine until the late 1980s. But when the Chinese stockpiles were exhausted, the demand for India's tigers increased. It appears that tiger bones are valued at 10 times more than tiger skins. The bones are ground up and made into 'tonic wine' and 'medicine'. It is estimated that the price of a tiger at its final destination is about $30,000. The poacher in the field receives about $400.

The Ranthambhore tigers never fail to surprise. They appear to have an in-built resilience; new tigers pop-up in unexpected places. On the 16th December, while surveying the buffer area from a lodge balcony, we heard a few children talking excitedly. It transpired that they had been grazing cattle on the hill behind the lodge and had wandered into a nala. Three shapes had suddenly burst forth from the grass in front of them and had run away at speed. Were they tigers? They were, asserted the children. How did they know? Well, they just knew. Further conversation was difficult for having settled on tigers they were determined to be stubborn. The animals could have been leopards. In any case, the three big creatures were never sighted again.

There was no doubt about the tiger seen in August 1991. A young male was spotted several times in the gardens of hotels and offices, and once even visited the Project Tiger complex. One night he entered the garden of a lodge, slept for a while, and then tried to take a look inside. The next morning, he was found strolling on the outskirts of the nearby town of Sawai Madhopur. When alerted, the park officials and the police found the tiger on a track, dozing, having brought all traffic to a stop and attracted a crowd of several hundred people. When he awoke and found himself the centre of incredulous attention, he bounded off into a field and took refuge under a bush. With some difficulty, the young male was tranquillised with a dart and taken to the park. He took a long time to come around - about nine hours in fact - and then disappeared. Surprisingly he was never sighted again.

Beyond Nalghati Valley, the track cuts through picturesque forest before it comes to more open vistas. Over the years, a tigress has been seen there, albeit infrequently. The forest rest house of Lahapur is not too far away so she goes by the name of Lahapur Female. In the winter, the Lahapur Female sprang a surprise, for she was seen with two cubs. There were only three reported sightings of the family, all from different and unrelated sources. There must have also been a tigress sandwiched between Lahapur Female and Nalghati Beti, for a few kilometres beyond Nalghati Valley the omnipresent Ashoka was once seen courting a totally different female.

Bakola Ben's sleep is over. She stirs and commences grooming, followed by a number of yawns.

There was also an unidentified male tiger who popped up at three different places in the course of the season and so livened up things a bit. On the 21st December he appeared as if from nowhere at the border of the home ranges of Noorjahan and Nalghati Beti. A look at a tourist's photograph showed a very young adult, but detailed identification was not possible. A similar tiger had previously been sighted feeding on a chital's leg in Nalghati Valley. In February, the mysterious male turned up at the lakes, picked up a dead langur monkey and disappeared into Jalra Forest. Perplexingly, he appeared to be quite familiar with the area and was tolerant of vehicles. He must have been adept at keeping out of Ashoka's way, for it is unlikely that the huge male would have knowingly tolerated his presence. Finally, in March, the same tiger turned up at Malik Lake where he demolished a sambar. He was a strange transient male who posed many questions.

The morning of the 12th April ushered in a joyous surprise. At about 8 o'clock Bela, Laxmi's six year old daughter, was sighted walking on the far side of the track that bisects Bakola. She stayed in dense vegetation, head and shoulders visible. After a while, she stopped and turned back. This was a little unusual. She lowered her head, lifted up an object the size of a hare, resumed her walk and then reached a small clearing. That's when we saw a cub running up. She herself stopped at a cactus-like bush and deposited the cub she had been carrying under it. She paused for a few seconds and then carried on alone, leaping a cliff effortlessly to disappear from view.

We encountered Bela and her two month old cubs four days later. She was attempting to change dens but one of the cubs was in no mood for walking. She moved up a steep incline followed by one cub. However, she had to return to the nala below for the other cub had stayed put. Perhaps it was hungry. We could make out some suckling activity and after that nothing happened for a while. Then she ventured to climb up the slope again and this time both the cubs followed. By the time she got to the top, although it was only 9.30 a.m., it had become quite hot. She stayed with her cubs under the shade of a clump of bushes until 5 p.m. when she began her descent into the Berda nala. But this time neither of the cubs showed any inclination to follow her. She waited at the bottom for a while and, in true feline fashion, took a fifteen minute nap. Refreshed, she resumed her task, calling to her babies while ascending. This time she stood no nonsense from the cubs as she clasped her mouth around one of them and descended with it dangling helplessly. The other cub thought it best to follow its mother obediently. Bela thus reached the Berda nala, crossed it, and climbed up the hill on the other side to Semli where she herself had been born and brought up by Laxmi. In the fading light, the short procession duly dissolved into emptiness leaving a pang of nostalgia behind.

Tragedy was still in the air and it struck in early June. One of the cubs was found to be on its own, looking anaemic. The forest department was alerted and the cub was eventually taken to the Jogi Mahal rest house. Despite treatment, it died. Its mother and sibling were not seen for a long time and a thorough search followed. Thankfully, the tigress and her cub were found, roaming Bakola via inaccessible places, but looking healthy and fit.

Amidst all the despair and gloom, Noorjahan offered the greatest hope. Every two weeks she would emerge, walking the familiar trails, taking in all the three lakes. When crossing a track she would weave around excited tourists in jeeps without batting an eyelid. The queen would continue her walk, followed by the tin boxes on wheels. Excited tourists would point cameras and a few flashes would go off in broad daylight. A hat would fly, a lens would fall and happy faces would watch until, with a final glare, she chose to disappear. Such is the magnetic power of a tigress in the wild.

Daku, the resident male of Bakola-Lakarda area, enjoys a soak in a shady waterhole on an April morning. Though tigers have ranged throughout the Asian tropics in recent times, being northern in origin they have an aversion to heat.

Postscript

THE FUTURE FOR TIGERS

In April 1993, visitors to Ramthambhore got a shock. At the height of the tourist season, the park was shut for eight days. As usual there was no notice, no explanation. But the reason leaked out. On April 13, forest guards had gone to make arrests in a nearby village where they suspected several people of selling the skin and bones of a newly poached tiger. The guards walked into an ambush and two were shot dead. Stunned and demoralized, their colleagues went on strike. For over a week the park was without protection. While the tourists were locked out, it was as if an open season for poachers had been declared.

With no tigers and a lot of tourist harassment, it was a sad time in Ranthambhore but the Forest Department didn't seem in the least bit concerned. It had reached the conclusion that encroachment, poaching and murder were not the main threats to the survival of Ranthambhore; they blamed the tourists, and banned entry to all private vehicles.

Instead, a fleet of canters - noisy, badly-sprung diesel lorries with open air bench seating - sped visitors around a pre-defined circuit in job lots of 25. We tried this out; A tiger wasn't sighted. Not for one whole week. Perhaps a cattle truck is not the best way of finding a tiger but there was enough evidence to suggest that there were hardly any tigers anyway. It was an experience to be endured, not enjoyed. Many tourists, on a once in a lifetime trip to see Ranthambhore's celebrated tigers, were dismayed.

A report critical of Forest Department policy remarked acidly that 'it is much easier to prevent a few cars entering the park and claim a victory for ecology, than to stop illegal grazing, wood-cutting and poaching'. This policy seems to have been wholeheartedly adopted. It may prove to be too successful; tourist numbers have dropped and are expected to fall even further. Park officials may soon be spared the bother of both tourists and tigers.

Tigers in Crisis

The tiger crisis was broken to the world at the International Tiger Symposium held in New Delhi in February 1993. On this 20th anniversary, a review of Project Tiger was published. It made for chilling reading; there is 'acute biotic pressure in Simlipal, sandalwood smuggling in Bandipur, Marijuana crops in Corbett, dam-building at Buxa, iron-ore mining at Indravati, terrorist gangs have shut down Nagarjunasagar and Manas, the tiger population has plummeted in Dudwa, poaching is rampant in Sariska...' It immediately spawned a flurry of diplomatic initiatives, a few of which appeared to hold out some hope. One of these was the demand by the standing committee of CITES (the Convention on International Trade in Endangered Species) which required trading countries to close down their markets in tiger bones and parts. Unfortunately, CITES cannot operate in six important tiger-range countries - Cambodia, Bhutan, North Korea, Laos, Myanmar (Burma) and Vietnam - as they are not parties to the convention. The U.S. declared its intention to invoke trade sanctions against China and Taiwan. India and China agreed the wording of a protocol that would squeeze the life from the trade.

The countries that have a native tiger population agreed to form a Global Tiger Forum to share information on poachers, smuggling and protection methods and to this end agreed to hold a meeting in early September 1993 in New Delhi. Two days before the conference opened, two men were arrested in a midnight raid in Delhi, following a four-month sting operation by TRAFFIC-India, which had infiltrated India's most active wildlife smuggling gang. Nearly

A striking view of Padam Lake as the sun sets behind the hills surrounding Ranthambhore.

Noorjahan grimaces in annoyance. Intent on catching a fleeing chital, Noorjahan got separated from her brother and mother. Lost, she looked around and repeatedly called hoping to establish contact. But her anxious appeals changed to a fierce snarl when she spotted us observing her.

200 kg. of tiger bones were impounded - all fresh, some with dried strands of meat still attached. A follow-up raid produced another 287 kg. Since an adult tiger has 10-16 kg. of bones, the first raid meant 13-20 adults and the second consignment at least 20. Estimates suggest that between 1990 and 1992 at least 500, and possibly 1000, tigers were poached in India.

Initiatives

The first meeting of the new Global Tiger Forum was held in Delhi on 3rd and 4th March 1994. Ten nations which still have wild tigers, including the normally isolationist Myanmar (Burma), met at ministerial level to discuss tiger protection, but China, North Korea and Laos did not attend. Predictably, the statement approved by the Delhi meeting called for several well-intentioned conservation measures. But surprisingly, the forum also set up a participatory trust fund to secure international finance.

In late 1994, at the CITES meeting in Fort Lauderdale, Florida, most countries with wild tiger populations, including China and India, pledged to stop the trade in tiger derivatives and to eliminate the use of tiger bones in traditional medicine. On 2nd March 1995, India and China signed their first ever animal conservation agreement - The Indo-China Protocol on the Conservation of the Tiger - which made many promises.

1996 and Beyond

In order to assess the impact of such initiatives, it is best to take stock and look at the current wild tiger situation with emphasis on India which still has the majority of the world's surviving tigers. An all-India census carried out in 1993 indicated 3,750 tigers in India, with 1,266 in the Project Tiger Reserves. However, due to the inaccuracies of the counting method, particularly the tendency to double-count, and the desire to present the tiger situation in a favourable light, the population was probably 1,000 individuals less at 2,750. Since the census, the situation appears to have worsened. According to Tiger Link, a coalition of conservation bodies in India, at least one tiger a day is being killed to supply the trade in tiger skin and bones. Today, it would appear that there are less than 2,500 wild tigers left in India. Since the 1996 world tiger population is around 4,000, India's population is nearly two thirds of the world's tigers. Tiger populations in Siberia, China, Indo-China, Sumatra and elsewhere are fragmented and under at least as much pressure as in India. If tigers cannot be saved in India, then they probably can't be saved at all.

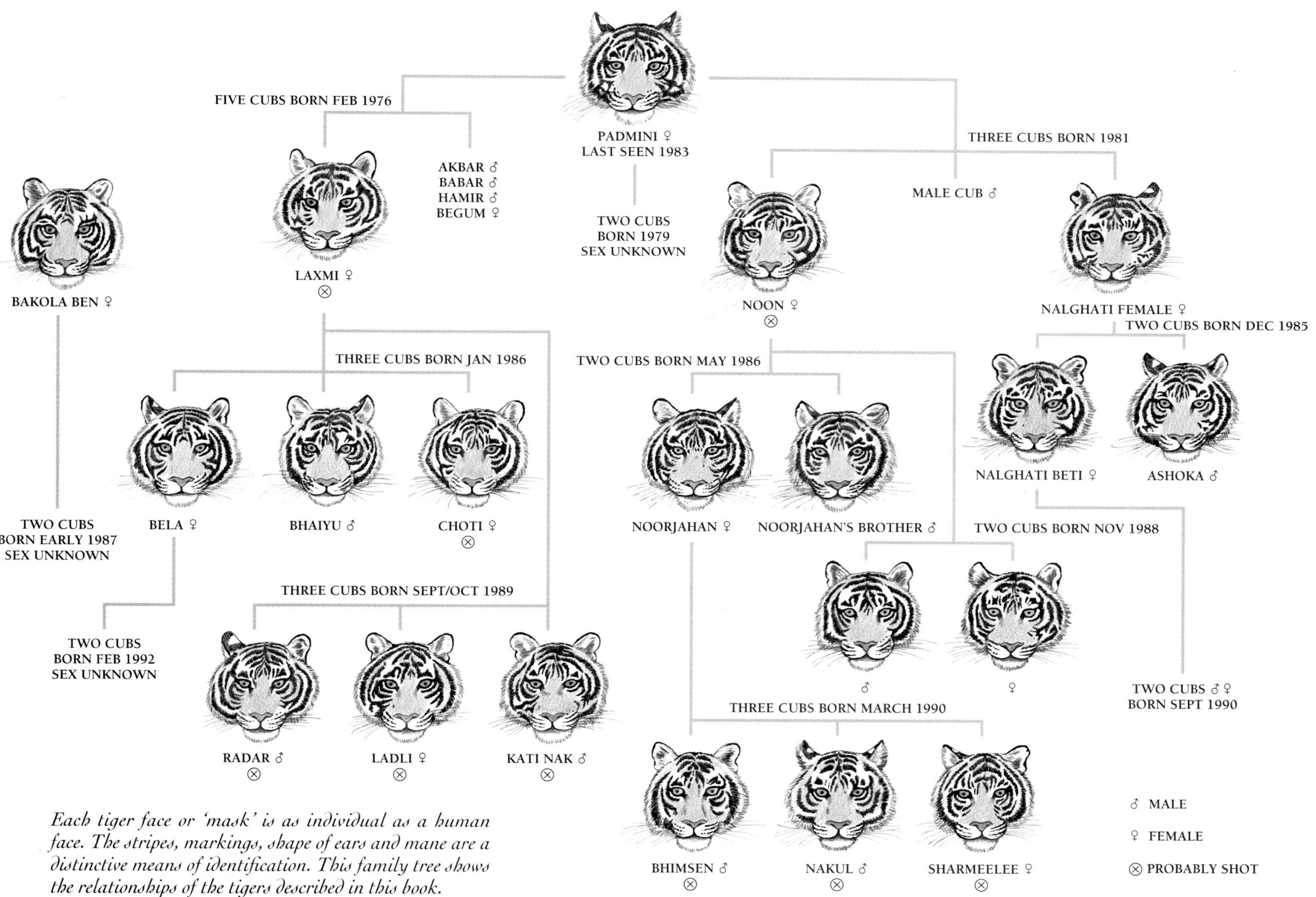

Each tiger face or 'mask' is as individual as a human face. The stripes, markings, shape of ears and mane are a distinctive means of identification. This family tree shows the relationships of the tigers described in this book.

India's vast human population is still growing at 2% per annum. India's economy is growing at an even faster rate. Not surprisingly, India's forests are disappearing. The tigers are finding fewer places in which to live, breed and hide. The long term fate of the tiger looks very grim. Yet that prediction may turn out to be irrelevant since the short term fate looks almost hopeless.

The problem, of course, is poaching. As China grows wealthier and as its population expands, the demand for tiger products will increase. Stacked against this relentless increase in demand, India's conservation efforts appear puny. True enough, TRAFFIC - India (an offshoot of WWF, the World Wide Fund for Nature) is backed by the Indian Ministry of Environment and Forests and together they are attempting to crack down on the poachers. But the poaching still continues.

Today, in the entire world, there are no tiger sub-populations estimated to contain more than 250 mature individual tigers. Approximately 95% of the tiger populations throughout the world are comprised of fewer than 120 tigers. Scientists have worked out that three additional years of moderate poaching, say 10% per year, would lead to a probability of extinction of greater than 95%. In the next few years the remaining tiger populations could easily fall beyond any possibility of recovery.

We would then enter the 21st century facing the virtual extinction of the wild tiger and with a sad shake of our heads, have to acknowledge that the only place to see the tiger would be in zoos.

Above: An encounter with Noorjahan walking along a vehicle track.

Right: Choti, on her way to the Kala Pathar Nala, stops to scan for prey on a misty Ranthambhore morning. Mists are infrequent in Ranthambhore, occurring only in winter, but whenever they appear, like the tiger, they lend a romantic dimension to an exotic land.

Tiger Photography

THE TECHNIQUES AND PROBLEMS OF PHOTOGRAPHING TIGERS

Tiger Tracking

Before you can photograph tigers you have to find them. Half of the skills concerning tiger photography in the wild have to do with tracking the elusive predator. We had a head start in Ranthambhore where tiger density was high and the terrain relatively open. But the essential problem remained: tigers chose not to show themselves. However, there were a few tricks we employed to increase our chances of finding the big cat. Unlike on the plains of East Africa, where the visual sense is of primary importance in finding a big cat, in Ranthambhore Forest it is the sense of hearing that is of paramount importance. The idea is to tap into the visual senses of the other denizens of the forest. The Sambar deer, for instance, emits an unmistakable call when it spots danger so that locating the source of the call puts you, hopefully, in the vicinity of a tiger. A Langur monkey, commanding a wide view atop a tall tree, also barks out an alarm when it spots danger. Less reliable, but still worth checking out, are calls of Chital deer. Chital are quite nervous animals and tend not to spare their vocal energies. Less reliable are peafowl calls. They are noisy birds but do call out with extra alarm if they manage to spot a tiger before it is too late.

Notwithstanding the above remarks, visual sense is sometimes important in locating a tiger. If you can locate a vulture or a tree-pie bird with a blood-smeared beak then the chances are that they have been uninvited guests at a tiger kill in the vicinity. (In fact, the picture on page 45 of Bela and Choti was made possible in this way). Again, if you spot a crow repeatedly diving into tall grass, you can be half-certain that it is purloining pieces of flesh from a kill (such crow behaviour made the picture on page 107 possible). Watching a deer staring into a thicket is a clue worth looking into. And if more animals join in the staring, then there is a good chance of finding a concealed predator. Driving about in Ranthambhore, one is also on the lookout for tiger footprints on the dirt-track. Following the footprints sometimes helps in narrowing down the area within which to search for the owner of the footprint. (See the photograph on page 119 of Noorjahan and her cubs which resulted from the lead given by the family's footprints.) Sometimes you get lucky and are able to directly pick out a tiger (photograph of Noorjahan on page 21). Even rarer are the instances when you stop to investigate the smell reaching your nostrils - tiger spray marks have a pungent smell, especially strong when fresh. (photographs of Bhaiyu on page 47 are the only instance where we have located a tiger in this way).

Mobile Photographic Hides

Having located the tigers, you want them to stay around - the last thing you want is a tiger disappearing into the thicket. Many early attempts at photographing tigers failed simply because the naturally wary tiger sped away. Fortunately for us, the tigers of Ranthambhore had got accustomed to four-wheel drives by the time we started our photography. The habituation had been surprisingly quick, a matter of only three to four years. Although the tigers got used to vehicles (they remained totally wild of course) they remained suspicious of people outside of vehicles. Thus, for example, when a forest tracker went walking through the forest, any tiger spotting him from afar would promptly head - literally - for the hills (matters would have been vastly different had a tracker accidentally stumbled onto a tiger, thereby cutting out its escape route). Incidentally, we have noticed the same aversion to humans on the plains of Africa where a big cat, as soon as it picks out a walking tribesperson from afar, slinks away, not even pausing to spray our car in its customary manner. Incidentally, big cats do distinguish between a vehicle and its occupants: they often sprayed our car but never us; on seeing a pet animal, a monkey or a dog, cheetahs in Kenya would eagerly try to prise open a closed car window seeing them as prey.

Capturing an intimate moment in the shade of the afternoon heat with a long telephoto lens.

So a vehicle served as a hide, and a mobile one at that, for us to photograph the Ranthambhore tigers. We used an open jeep and avoided making sudden movements and doing silly things like standing upright. Camouflage was not necessary but, interestingly, the Forest Department in South India forbids the use of white vehicles in its parks since it is believed that elephants charge at them (they are thought to run away from coloured vehicles).

Readiness

Photographing tigers in a straightforward way is relatively easy once they have been located and they choose to stay. This is because long periods of inactivity are interspersed with very short bursts of action (an example of this is the sequence of Bhaiyu chasing a mongoose on page 53). So all you have to do is to be ready and the thought to have uppermost in mind is to not fluff any opportunity that might arise.

Conduct in the Field

It is a simple truth, often forgotten, that in order to photograph natural behaviour of tigers, you need the tigers to behave. The relevant point here is that old wisdom: the observer affects the observed. The adverse effect of observing, both from the tiger's and the photographer's point of view, can be reduced by better conduct. For example, if on spotting a tiger you drive fast and in a straight line towards the cat then the chances are that it will disappear into places that your vehicle can't go. You are also likely to frighten the cat if you drive too close to it. It was for this reason that we used long telephoto lenses - initially a Canon 500mm FD and later a Canon 600mm EF when autofocus camera systems made their debut (the photograph of Noon's family on page 37 was made possible with the 500mm lens and that of Laxmi's family on page 79 with the 600mm). Another advantage of a long telephoto is that when the occasion arises, you can get a tight close-up with impact (see the photographs of Choti and Bela submerged in water on page 41 and a reclining Bakola Ben on page 55). Such shots are pleasing for the intimacy they impart.

Even if you behave well, the behaviour of other humans is out of your control. You can either give in to photographer's rage or quietly get on with photography. Attitude is important in wildlife photography. When we come across Daku, enjoying a lie-in in a pool, we had to be careful and patient in order to induce the misanthropic monarch to stay on. Once he had accepted our presence and relaxed, we quickly composed and took a couple of pictures (see page 41) before the noise of an approaching vehicle disturbed him - he rose and left without ceremony. Although there is some exhilaration in being able to document, it is short-lived; the creative in you wants to do more than that.

Creative freedom

When photographing wild tigers, the degrees of creative freedom are few. For instance, the photograph of Noon's cubs walking along the lake shore on page 101 was taken from the opposite shore with a 600mm lens plus a 1.4x extender. Our only creative freedom was to slightly under-expose in order to enhance the colour of the evening light. However, one way of increasing creative freedom is by anticipating. Another method of increasing creative freedom is by reacting faster. We were thus able to take the photograph of Nalghati Female and Ashoka on page 20, initially with several focal lengths, before settling on a 300mm focal length to capture the delicate forest light falling on the vibrant-looking tigers. Sometimes, you are given creative freedom on a plate. When Choti climbed and sat on the tree, see page 44, she was relaxed and stayed. This behaviour enabled us to manoeuvre the jeep near her such that we could use a 24mm wide angle lens to include her environment. The light was appalling but there was time to compensate by over-exposing the film.

To impart the feel of the tiger's habitat, inclusion of its immediate environment in the picture is necessary. Thus the foilage in the viciously snarling Bhaiyu picture, page 48, enhances his menace. The picture of Bakola Ben on page 55, taken with a wide-angle lens, gives an added dimension to her daily life.

Finally

We have always been fascinated by big cats, tigers in particular, and we really enjoy wildlife photography. So for us, photographing tigers in the wild was like a great big love-affair. It may be that the magical ingredient that makes a photograph special results from such involvement. (perhaps the cover photograph and that on page 93 are examples of photographs with that touch). This opinion on photography is debatable, but what is not is the fact that we find photographing tigers an immensely pleasurable activity.

The tiger's love of water can with patience provide an opportunity to capture a scene such as this.

Tracking Tigers

THE TRAIL TO TIGER KNOWLEDGE

During our conversations with people associated with Ranthambhore, we were continually surprised by the diversity of knowledge and opinions expressed on tigers. Initially, we believed everything we heard but when we had time to digest, reflect and question, we made the effort to classify various sources of information into two categories: The park administrators appeared to have scant knowledge of tigers and were not interested in learning. The people in the field - the jeep drivers and the handful of trackers - had many interesting tiger encounters to relate, much of it useful, once we learnt to trim the exaggerations (and ignore accounts of personal valour). Nevertheless, for the academic in us, this knowledge was bitty and unconnected and we were aware that it could be misleading. We had to resist going from snapshot behaviour to the behaviour of tigers in general since the bridges between the two were missing in Ranthambhore. Surprisingly, no one has ever been permitted to carry out tiger research in Ranthambhore. By tiger research we mean building up tiger knowledge on the basis of a systematic study of a large number of tigers.

Studies of Tiger Anatomy

A first step in an objective study of tigers is its anatomy. This can be carried out far away from a tiger habitat, as long as there is a tiger carcass or a captive tiger to study. Sex difference, cub-adult differences, differences among subspecies and so on can also be analysed with a collection of captive tigers. Not surprisingly, tiger anatomy was being actively studied as early as the 19th century and today it is well-researched. But it still leaves most tiger behaviour to the imagination.

Accounts of Hunters

Tigers in the wild have been hunted either for sport or because a few of them became man-eaters. Some of the early hunters were good observers and were also able to accurately relate their experiences. We thus gained some idea of tiger behaviour in the wild. But there was a lot lacking in such observations: they were really bits and pieces of information of an elusive predator on the run. In addition, the behaviour of man-eating tigers was likely to be different from the rest of the wild population. As a result the accounts of the hunters were absorbing but misleading, even if one toned down the obvious exaggerations. We inherited an inaccurate image of the wild tiger.

Systematic Field Work

To properly learn tiger behaviour in the wild, you have to leave your zoo, museum or laboratory, go into the wild and stay there for a long time. Such laborious field studies of tigers did not begin until the 1960s. They commenced with George Schaller's year-long work in central India in 1967 and ushered in an era of rigorous academic work on tigers. The rigour is characterised by the painstaking collection of a huge amount of data on a large number of tigers. Field studies also introduced ecology into the portrait of the wild tiger since data was collected on the tiger's environment - the researchers noted down preferred resting sites of tigers, ambush points, location of den sites and so on - and analysis was carried out to see how the tiger's behaviour related to its habitat. Schaller's study did a lot to alter the image of the wild tiger. In particular, the tiger became inseparable from its environment.

Radio Telemetry

Schaller employed simple tools - pen, paper and binoculars. Then, in the early 1970s, dart guns, radio collars and radio tracking equipment were introduced. Using such sophisticated equipment, Seidensticker, Sunquist and other researchers began a long term study of tigers in Chitwan National Park, Nepal. The equipment employed made it relatively easy to monitor the movements of radio-collared tigers by day and night. The value of such monitoring can be seen in mapping out the home range. By making repeated observations on the movements of tigers, researchers could demarcate home ranges of tigers and also ascertain the extent of overlap, if any. By encompassing ecology and human settlements pressing on the park, the Chitwan Tiger Project has also been comprehensive. While it has altered our image of the tiger once again - in particular that wild tigers co-exist uneasily with rural populations - it remains to be seen if the research can be used to save the tiger.

Satellites and Computers

To save the gravely endangered tiger, we need to compile an inventory of the remaining suitable tiger habitats. Scientific research on tigers is at last compiling such a list. Scientists are currently putting information gathered by satellites on tiger habitats through powerful computers to build comprehensive data files on actual and potential tiger habitats.

We also need to know how many wild tigers currently exist. To this end, researchers in the field are refining counting methods so that accurate tiger censuses can be carried out. While this methodological research is laudable, the practical problem of counting the world's tigers depends upon securing funds to implement the newer methods.

DNA Testing

With blood and skin samples of different tigers, researchers in laboratories can now tell how tigers are related. If they are closely related, then it is likely that inbreeding occurred. This could mean that such a tiger population is vulnerable to infectious diseases but scientists are not in agreement on this implication. Some scientists believe that genetic variability makes little difference to conservation and is, therefore, not essential. But suppose that there is an outbreak of an infectious virus and it is decided to translocate tigers at risk. The logistics of such an operation could face severe practical problems: safety of tigers, skilled manpower, funds, goodwill and so on.

Captive Breeding Programmes

Zoo biologists have been remarkably successful in breeding tigers in captivity. Advances have also been made in producing 'test-tube' tigers. The value of such programmes lies in having healthy captive tigers should they be wiped out in the wild. Presumably, the captive tigers are then meant to be released into the wild. While such intentions are noble, it has not been made clear how tigers might be released into the wild. Will there be any wilderness areas left in which to release the tigers? Would the forces threatening tigers in the wild have been eliminated? Would the tigers survive? Would they breed? Would they be too successful and eat up the entire available prey?

Research and Tiger Crisis

There is little doubt that research on tigers is advancing and adding to our knowledge. However, all the research being carried out may make little difference to the fate of the tiger. The reasons are practical. Excellent research takes a long time and even longer to implement, given real life difficulties. The wild tiger however is in serious danger of extinction and does not have the luxury of time. To most interested people it is obvious that the sure way to save the wild tiger is to save its habitat. We have had a perfect ready-made legacy of tiger habitats and it is sensible to simply look after this inheritance. No amount of fascinating research will alter that policy conclusion. To save habitats you need political will. It is as simple as that.

Index